MW00635313

A Rendezvous With Colorado History

By:
Dorothy Dutton Ed.D.
and
Caryl Humphries M.A.

© 1999 by Sterling Ties Publications, L.L.P.
All Rights Reserved
2nd Printing 2001
Revised 2004

Cover Design by: Murie Graphic Design
Drawings by: Mary Coyle, Hans Schnackenberg, and Dorothy Dutton
All photos not credited were taken by the authors

ISBN O-9642420-2-8

400020085

Printed in the United States of America

Published by:
Sterling Ties Publications
5989 Sterling Drive
Boise, Idaho 83703
208-853-0507
sterling5989@msn.com
www.sterlingties.com

A Word of Thanks

Writing an overview of the history of Colorado is much more difficult than we originally anticipated. As we did our research, we found that there were many different stories about Colorado. Some were true, and some weren't. Other stories, no one really knows about for sure. We have tried to make this book as accurate as possible. If there is any information that is not correct, we take full responsibility. If you question the accuracy of anything in this book, we would appreciate hearing from you.

This book could not have been written without the help and support of many people. It would be hard to name everyone who helped, but we would like to try to thank some of the many people who helped to make this book possible.

Thank you to the following people for reading the book and helping us to make it more historically accurate:

Dr. Duane Vandenbusche - History Professor at Western State College

C.J. Brafford - Director of the Ute Indian Museum in Montrose

Teachers and administrators from throughout the state read the book and gave us very helpful feedback. We would like to thank:

Sue Friehauf (Fort Collins), Linda Jones (Littleton), Wayne Stone (Hygiene), Annie Hannagan (Hygiene), Teresa Stamp (Hygiene), Pat Chambers (Dillon), Carol Rush (Laporte), Vic Smith (Fort Collins), Brian Carpenter (Fort Collins), Bridgette Sanderford (Montrose), Liz Stansberry (Denver), Ron Maulsby (Fort Collins), Camille Agone (Dillon), and Susan Lebow (Gunnison)

Special thanks to:

Fred Brown, who was not only the model for our Mr. Brown, but a great source of information and inspiration.

We would also like to thank:

The people at the Colorado State Historical Library in Denver

Melinda Terry for her help in finding information about the hairstreak butterfly .

Last, but not least, we would like to thank our family for their love and support. We dedicate this book to them:

Ed, Kelsey, and Gania Humphries

Fred, Gania, Abigail, Timothy, and Chris Brown

Tom, Debbie, Erin, and Michael Dutton

About the Authors

Caryl Humphries

Caryl has been an elementary school teacher for 17 years, including one year in Colorado. The past 14 years she has taught fourth grade at Eagle Elementary in Eagle, Idaho. She received her B.A. from the University of Northern Colorado and holds a masters in reading education from Boise State University. Caryl has coordinated the fourth grade Rendezvous held in the Meridian School District for the last 14 years. She lives in Boise with her husband, Ed, and two daughters, Kelsey and Gania. This book was co-written with her mother, Dorothy Dutton.

Dr. Dorothy Dutton

Dorothy is an educational consultant and reading specialist. She holds a masters degree in elementary education from Western State College in Colorado and a doctorate in reading from the University of Northern Colorado. Dorothy has a total of thirty-three years of teaching experience. She has taught every level from kindergarten through college. She was district curriculum director in the Gunnison School District for three years. When she retired from teaching, Dorothy moved to Idaho from Colorado to be near her daughter and family. She has four children and seven grandchildren.

Table of Contents

Introduction
A Rendezvous With
Colorado History

It was a warm sunny September day. All of the students at Oak Grove Elementary School were settling into their new classes. Mr. Brown's class said the Pledge of Allegiance. Then they all sat in their seats.

"Welcome back to school," said Mr. Brown. "I hope that you had a good summer vacation. We have an exciting year ahead of us. We'll be learning lots of new things."

Brooke raised her hand. "I can't wait to learn all about Colorado history. My sister said that it is the best thing about your class."

Mr. Brown agreed, "Colorado history is my favorite subject, too."

"I already know a lot about Colorado," stated Michael. "My grandmother told me that the dome on the capitol building is solid gold."

"The dome is not solid gold, but it is covered with gold, Michael," said Mr. Brown. "About 200 ounces of pure gold leaf covers the dome. They have had to put new gold leaf on the dome three times. The last time was in 1993. Does anyone know anything else that is special about our capitol building?"

"It looks like the capitol building in Washington D.C." said Kelsey.

"You are right, Kelsey," said Mr. Brown. "Our Colorado capitol building is very similar in design to the nation's capitol.

"There is something else that is special about our capitol building. Most of the materials used to build it came from right here in Colorado. The outside walls are granite which came from near *Gunnison*. The rose onyx you will see inside the building on the walls and the pillars was found near *Beulah*. Rose onyx is a very rare marble and has not been found anywhere else in the world. Almost all of the rose onyx found was used to complete the capitol building.

"The sandstone which was used for the foundations came from near *Fort Collins*. The marble floors and stairs are made from very special marble that comes from a place near *Marble*, Colorado. This marble was also used for the Lincoln Memorial and the Tomb of the Unknown Soldier in Washington D.C.

"We will be learning many more interesting things about Colorado this year. I have lots of exciting things to share with you about our rich history. I know that you will really enjoy learning about our state. Why don't I pass out your history books. You can begin looking at them while I give you your other books. Later we will begin to look at some of the things that make Colorado so special."

Mr. Brown began to pass out the books.

Chapter 1
Symbols of Colorado

A few days later Mr. Brown's class noisily returned from lunch. Mr. Brown put his finger to his lips. The students began to quiet down. "How did you know that I wanted you to quit talking?" asked Mr. Brown.

"You put your finger on your lips. That means to be quiet," answered Abigail.

"You're right. A finger on the lips is a **symbol** that almost everyone knows."

"What do you mean by symbol, Mr. Brown?" asked Bryan.

"A symbol is a picture, object, or action that stands for something else. When we said the pledge this morning we were looking at another symbol. The United States flag is a symbol of our country. Each star on the flag stands for one of the fifty states. The thirteen stripes stand for the thirteen original colonies. The colors on the flag are also important. White stands for purity, blue for justice, and red for courage."

The United States flag is a symbol of our country.

"I never knew the flag stood for that many things," said Kevin.

"Can anyone think of another symbol?" asked Mr. Brown.

"Would the golden arches be a symbol?" asked Tim.

"Good example," Mr. Brown laughed. "What do you think about when you see them?"

"Hamburgers!" shouted Yeong Se.

"McDonald's!" exclaimed Michael.

"The golden arches are a symbol that people all over the world know. We see symbols every day in many different places.

"Throughout history the people of Colorado have

The golden arches are a symbol most boys and girls know. *(Courtesy: McDonald's Corporation)*

chosen things they feel represent our special state. Several of these symbols have been adopted by the state **legislature**."

"I've heard the word legislature before, but I really don't know what it means," said Gania.

"There are three parts, or branches, of our government. The executive branch is the governor of our state or the president of our country. The judicial branch is the judges and the courts. The judicial branch makes sure that the laws or rules we live by are obeyed. They also make sure that the laws are fair. The legislature is the third branch of government. It is an important group of men and women. They are elected by the people of the state. The legislature makes the laws and many decisions about how the state should be run.

"One decision the legislature makes is to decide which symbols best represent Colorado. The symbols they choose are called official symbols. Today we are going to learn about Colorado's official symbols."

The State Seal

"One symbol that every state has is a state seal. This seal is used on all important state papers. It shows that something is official or that it belongs to that state.

"When Colorado became a state, they decided to use the seal that was designed for the territory. They only changed two things. They placed the words STATE OF COLORADO on the top of the seal. They also put the date 1876 on the bottom because this was the year that Colorado became a state. This new seal was approved as the state seal of Colorado on March 15, 1877."

"What does the state seal look like?" asked Joe.

"It is a round shape that is 2 ½ inches wide. At the top of the seal is the eye of God within a triangle. Under the triangle is a bundle of elm rods and a battle ax. The bundle is tied with a red, white, and blue band. The words UNION AND CONSTITUTION are on the band.

"Under this is a shield. The top part of the shield is red with three snow capped mountains and clouds. On the bottom part of the shield are some tools used in mining. Under the shield is a white band with the motto ***NIL SINE NUMINE*** which means 'nothing without **providence**.' Around the

Lewis Ledyard Weld helped to design Colorado's State Seal.
(Credit: Colorado Historical Society C.H.S.)

10

The seal of the state of Colorado is used on all official papers.
(Courtesy: Colorado Secretary of State)

outside of the seal is a red band with the words STATE OF COLORADO on the top and the date 1876 at the bottom."

"What does providence mean?" asked Kelsey.

"The word 'providence' means divine guidance. The people who chose this motto must have wanted to say that our state would not do anything without being led by God," said Mr. Brown.

"Who designed the state seal for Colorado?" asked Ed.

"The person who is mostly responsible is **Lewis Ledyard Weld. Abraham Lincoln** chose him to be the Territorial Secretary for Colorado in July of 1861. Some say that the Territorial Governor **William Gilpin** also helped to design the seal."

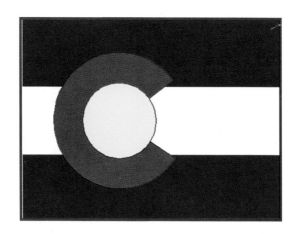

The State Flag

"Can anyone think of another symbol of Colorado?" asked Mr. Brown.

"Would our state flag be one?" asked Paul.

"Yes," responded Mr. Brown. "Can anyone tell us what our flag looks like?"

"It has a large red letter 'C' with a gold circle inside the 'C'," said Brink.

"That is correct," praised Mr. Brown. "The letter 'C' stands for Colorado. It is in red to represent the red soil of the state. The gold circle stands for the gold mined here. Gold mining has been very important to Colorado's history. What else do you see on the flag?"

"The background has three stripes," said Kelli. "They look like they are the same size. The top and the bottom ones are blue and the middle one is white."

"Great," said Mr. Brown. "The blue stripes stand for Colorado's blue skies. The white one represents the snow for which our state is famous."

"Mr. Brown, I noticed that there are two cords that are attached to the Colorado flag. One of them is gold and the other is silver. Do they stand for the gold and silver that has been mined in our state?" asked Nicole.

"I am not sure," replied Mr. Brown, "but that would be my guess. I do know that our flag was designed by ***Andrew Carlisle Johnson*** in 1911."

The Colorado Blue Spruce

Mr. Brown paused for a moment and then picked up a picture from his desk. "Does anyone know what this is?" he asked.

"Sure, it is a big pine tree," said Zach.

"That is a good guess, but actually it is not a pine, it is a type of spruce tree," said Mr. Brown. "This is a very special kind of tree to Colorado. It is the **Colorado blue spruce**. It was first discovered on **Pikes Peak** in 1862. In 1939, the legislature adopted this tree as our state tree."

"How can you tell that it is a Colorado blue spruce?" asked Kate.

"Each type of tree has things that make it different. The Colorado blue spruce grows at elevations of 5,000 to 11,000 feet. The color of the tree ranges from green to blue to true silver. Sometimes this tree is called the silver spruce. The new growth of this tree is more bluish than the older part of the branches. The blue and silver colors are from a bloom or powder on the needles. This powder wears off as the year goes on. Older trees are often dark green.

"The sharp needles are about an inch long and are usually a dull blue-green. This tree has a rough brown bark. The light brown cones grow up to four inches in length. The Colorado blue spruce makes a beautiful Christmas tree."

The Colorado blue spruce grows throughout Colorado's high mountains.

Pikes
Peak

The Lark Bunting

The lark bunting sometimes sings while it flies.
(Credit: C.H.S.)

"Do we have a state bird?" asked Jessie.

"Oh yes," said Mr. Brown. "Does anyone know what it is?"

"It is the **lark bunting**," said Nicole proudly.

"How did you know that?" questioned Mr. Brown.

"My grandfather is an expert on them. He studies them all the time," she replied.

"What can you tell us about them?" Mr. Brown asked.

"The male bird is black with white patches and white edges on his wings and tail. In the winter, he changes to almost the same color as the female bird, except his chin and tummy stay the same color. The female lark bunting is gray brown on top and white on her tummy.

"The male lark bunting gets to be about this long," said Nicole as she held her hands about seven inches apart. "The female is a little smaller.

"In September, they fly south for the winter. Did you know that the lark bunting even sings while it is flying? Grandpa says that lark buntings must think Colorado is pretty special, because they come back here every spring."

"Wow, Nicole! That was great!" exclaimed Mr. Brown. "I don't think your grandfather is the only expert on lark buntings. Thank you for sharing all of that with us.

"Did you know that lark buntings live mostly in flocks or groups in the plains regions and places over 8,000 feet in elevation?" asked Mr. Brown. "They eat grasshoppers and waste grain. Since grasshoppers are harmful to crops, farmers think of the lark bunting as a friend.

"It is an interesting story about how the lark bunting became our state bird. Colorado held a vote to choose a state bird. The meadowlark was chosen as the most popular bird in Colorado. Later, a second vote was taken and the mountain bluebird was chosen. Finally, the Colorado Audubon Society told the legislature that since the meadowlark and the bluebird were already state birds of other states, the lark bunting would be a better choice. The legislature voted to make the lark bunting our state bird on April 29, 1931."

Colorado has laws which protect the columbine in the wild.
(Courtesy: Nancy Swille)

The Columbine

"We also have a state flower," continued Mr. Brown. "It is the white and lavender-blue *columbine*. This color of columbine was chosen as the state flower because it represents the blue skies, the white snow, and the yellow gold found in our state.

"The columbine grows wild throughout Colorado. We have laws that protect our state flower. The name columbine probably was chosen because its flowers look like circles of little doves. The word for dove in Latin is columbae. The columbine became our state flower on April 4, 1899."

Blue Grama Grass

"We even have a state grass," added Mr. Brown. "***Blue Grama grass*** grows throughout Colorado. This grass has short curly leaves. It is native to Colorado which means it has always grown here. It was adopted as our state grass on May 20, 1987.

"Blue grama grass begins growing in the spring and has a deep root system. This allows it to grow in very dry areas. It grows to be about five inches tall. The blue grama is a perennial which means it comes back every year. This grass can survive fire, a long drought, or severe cold. Blue grama, which helped make the sod on the eastern plains, can be found throughout the state."

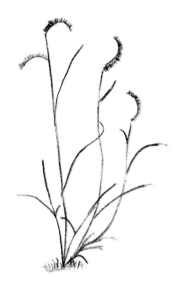

Blue grama grass is native to Colorado.

Rocky Mountain Big Horn Sheep

"Colorado has a state animal. I will give you some clues, and I want you to see if you can guess what it is. Are you ready?"

The whole class nodded their heads.

"O.K. This animal is found in the Rocky Mountains," began Mr. Brown.

"Is it a mountain lion?" asked Juan.

"Good guess, but that isn't our state animal. Let me give you some more clues. The male is about 3 to 3 ½ feet tall at the shoulders and weighs up to 300 pounds. The female is a little smaller. These large animals are known for their nimbleness and their great sense of balance. They have huge horns which curve backward from the forehead."

"I know," shouted Adam. "It is the ***Rocky Mountain big horn sheep.***"

"Right, Adam," answered Mr. Brown. "Did you know their horns can grow up to 50 inches long?

A Rocky Mountain big horn sheep's horns can grow up to 50" long.

15

Their large horns act like a football helmet and protect their heads and brains from injury when they butt heads. This is the way they fight. Some rams, or male sheep, have been seen to butt heads as many as 48 times in one day. The sound they make when they butt heads can be heard as much as a mile away."

"I saw some of them at the zoo in **Denver** when we visited there last summer," said Maria excitedly. "They can climb in really rocky areas. It was fun to watch them."

"We saw them near the top of Pikes Peak when we went up on the cog railway this last summer," said Mr. Brown. "The Rocky Mountain big horn sheep is protected by the state of Colorado. It was chosen as our state animal May 1, 1961."

The Stegosaurus

"Another animal, that lived in Colorado 150 million years ago, is our state fossil. The *stegosaurus* probably weighed ten tons. Its brain was about the size of a walnut and only weighed around 2 ½ ounces. A full grown stegosaurus would be about 30 feet long. There were four bony spikes at the end of its tail which were probably used for defense. The bony plates that came up from the spine may have been used as armor.

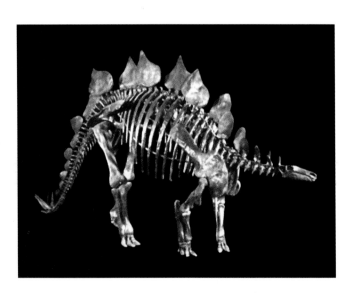

This stegosaurus skeleton is on display at the Denver Museum of Natural History.
(Credit: Denver Museum of Natural History)

"The teeth of the stegosaurus were quite weak so it probably ate only leaves or vegetation, and not meat. The front legs of the stegosaurus were shorter than the back legs and some scientists think that it may have stood up on its back legs to eat from the tops of the trees.

"A group of students from **McElwain Elementary School** in **Thorton** suggested that the stegosaurus should be our state fossil since the first complete skeleton was found right here in Colorado. **Governor Richard D. Lamm** made it official on April 28, 1982."

"I saw the skeleton of the stegosaurus at the Museum of Natural History in Denver. It was huge," said Keith. "A teacher and some students from **Cañon City High School** found the bones. It was so cool!"

Thorton Denver

• Cañon
City

The Aquamarine

"Why would anyone think a bunch of old bones are neat?" asked Erin.

"Well, maybe you would like our state gem better," smiled Mr. Brown. "Does anyone know what it is?"

"Is it a diamond?" asked Gania.

"No, but some people think it is just as pretty," said Mr. Brown. "The **aquamarine** was adopted as our state gemstone April 30, 1971. It is usually blue, blue-green, or green. The blue variety is the most valuable. The aquamarine is related to the emerald, but the emerald is much more valuable. **Mount Antero** and **White Mountain** are two of the best places for finding the gem aquamarine."

The aquamarine is used to make beautiful jewelry.
(Courtesy: Ed Humphries and Stewart's Gem Shop)

Yeong Se raised his hand. "Mr. Brown, isn't it time for music?"

"Oh, you are right," he said as he looked at the clock. "We can finish talking about our state symbols when you come back."

"Where the Columbines Grow"

As the class went into the music room, they were still talking about some of the symbols of Colorado.

"What are you all talking about?" asked Mrs. Mapp.

"Oh we are studying about Colorado history. Mr. Brown has been telling us about some of our state symbols," said Kelsey.

"How exciting. Did you know that Colorado also has a state song?" Mrs. Mapp asked.

"Really? Can you sing it for us, Mrs. Mapp?" asked Tim.

"Sure. I think I have a tape right here," said Mrs. Mapp. "Yes, here it is." She began to sing:

Where the snowy peaks gleam in the moonlight,
Above the dark forests of pine,
And the wild foaming waters dash onward,
Toward lands where the tropics stars shine;
Where the scream of the bold mountain eagle
Responds to the notes of the dove
Is the purple robed West, the land that is best,
The pioneer land that we love.

(Chorus)
Tis the land where the columbines grow,
Overlooking the plains far below,
While the cool summer breeze in the evergreen trees
Softly sings where the columbines grow.

The students practiced the song all period. When they returned to class Chelsea said, "Mr. Brown we have a surprise for you. Mrs. Mapp taught us the Colorado state song. It is called 'Where the Columbines Grow' **by A.J. Fynn**. Do you want to hear it?"

"You bet!" he said. When the class finished, Mr. Brown clapped. "That is super. You are great singers. Did you know that it was written in 1915 after Mr. Fynn had been on a camping trip? He wrote the song as a way of praising our beautiful state flower. The legislature voted that same year to make it our state song."

The Square Dance

"Are you as good at dancing as you are at singing?" asked Mr. Brown. "Our state also has a special dance.

Square dancing is enjoyed by many people.
(Courtesy: David Parker)

"On March 16, 1992, the legislature chose the *square dance* as the official folk dance. Americans have been doing square dances since 1651. The square dance is usually done with eight people standing in the shape of a square. There are two people on each side of the square. Some other types of dance are also called square dancing even though they may be done in lines or in a circle. Clogging, a type of dance done with heavy shoes, is also a type of square dancing. Mrs. Johnson is an expert on square dancing. I'll bet if we ask her she will teach us a dance or two in P.E. Right now let's learn more about some of our other state symbols."

The Greenback Cutthroat Trout

"How many of you have ever gone fishing?" Mr. Brown asked. Several hands went up. "We have a lot of wonderful fishing spots in our state. Many of our lakes and streams have different kinds of trout in them. The ***greenback cutthroat trout*** at one time lived in many small creeks, streams and rivers in Colorado. Then people started to move to Colorado and pollution from mining and other things began to kill this fish. People feared that the greenback cutthroat trout would soon become **extinct**."

"What does extinct mean?" asked Kelli.

"If they were extinct, that means there would no longer be any greenback cutthroat trout living on earth. They would all be dead," explained Mr. Brown. "In the early 1990s, scientists found some small groups of this fish living in ***Rocky Mountain National Park***. The greenback cutthroat is very rare, so scientists began to protect it. Someday soon, they hope to be able to move the greenback to other lakes and rivers throughout Colorado.

Rocky Mountain
National Park

"The cutthroat are the only native trout in our state. That means they were not brought to our state from somewhere else. You can tell the greenback cutthroat trout from other trout because of its light-colored body. Dark colored spots can be found on its back and on its sides near the tail. There is a crimson slash on each side of the throat under the jaw. It was adopted as our state fish on March 15, 1994."

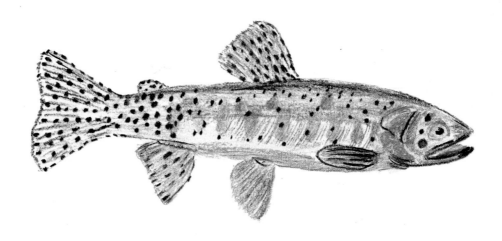

The greenback cutthroat trout is our state fish.

The Colorado Hairstreak Butterfly

"Two years later, on April 17, 1996, the legislature adopted a state insect, the **Colorado hairstreak butterfly.** Teacher **Melinda Terry**, of **Wheeling Elementary** in **Aurora**, and her fourth grade classes worked for several years to get the legislature to adopt this insect.

This female hairstreak butterfly is sitting on a Gambell's oak leaf.
(Credit: James A. Scott)

"The hairstreak is two inches wide and has purple wings with black borders. It also has large golden orange spots, usually two or three of them, in the outside corner of each wing. It is a blue gray underneath. It is easily identified because of its beautiful colors and the slender 'tail' that is part of the bottom wing.

"The Colorado hairstreak usually lives in the foothills or mountain canyons of southern Colorado. It is found at elevations of 6,500 to 7,500 feet. Our state butterfly likes to live in partly shaded areas but often sits on leaves which are in the sun.

"The Colorado hairstreak lays its eggs on the bark of the Gambell's oak. The oak is the main plant food for Colorado's state insect."

Students from at least 10 Colorado schools across the state came to ask the legislature to make the hairstreak butterfly the state insect.
(Courtesy: Melinda Terry)

Our Next Symbol?

"As we study about Colorado this year, we can all be looking for something special that we think might make a good symbol. If we have good reasons for our choice, we can present it to the legislature. It would really be fun if our class could suggest the next symbol of Colorado."

"I think that skiing should be the official sport of Colorado," suggested Lindsay.

"What a great idea!" agreed Mr. Brown. "We do not have a state sport. What do you think?"

The class all agreed.

"O.K. Then tonight, I want you to think of the reasons why you think skiing should be the state sport. Tomorrow we can write a letter to the legislature to see what we can do."

Aurora •

What Did You Learn?

1. What makes a symbol official?
2. Who are the two people who helped design the state seal of Colorado?
3. What is written on the red band around the outside edge of the state seal of Colorado?
4. What does the motto Nil Sine Numine mean?
5. Describe the Colorado state flag.
6. Where was the Colorado blue spruce first discovered?
7. What do the three colors of the columbine represent?
8. Why do Rocky Mountain big horn male sheep butt heads?
9. Who suggested that the stegosaurus become our state fossil? Why did they think this would be a good symbol?
10. Which color aquamarine is the most valuable?
11. What is the main food source for the hairstreak butterfly?
12. Who wrote the Colorado state song?

What Do You Think?

1. The greenback cutthroat trout was chosen as our state fish. Why do you think they chose this fish rather than a rainbow trout?
2. Do you think the Rocky Mountain big horn sheep was a good choice to represent Colorado? Why or why not?
3. If you could choose a new symbol for Colorado, what would you choose and why?
4. Why do you think Colorado has laws to protect the columbine?

Use Your Imagination

1. Imagine that you are a lark bunting. Tell about your trip as you fly south for the winter. Where will you go? How will it feel to fly so far? What will you see?
2. Pretend you are a Rocky Mountain big horn sheep. Where do you live? What do you like to do?
3. Write a letter to the legislature to convince them they should adopt a new symbol you have chosen. Make sure to include the reasons for your choice.
4. Write a story about what you think the earth was like when the stegosaurus was alive.

Colorado Landforms

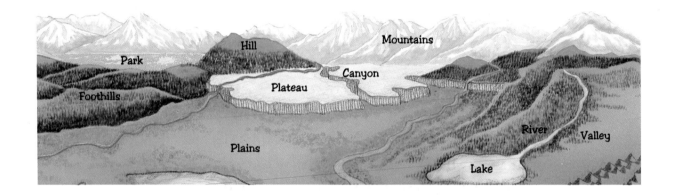

Canyon - a long narrow valley with steep sides

Foothills - hills near the bottom or foot of a mountain

Hill - an area of high land which is lower than a mountain

Lake - large body of water surrounded by land

Mountain - a natural raised part of the earth larger and higher than a hill

Mountain Range - a row or group of mountains

Park - an area of high flat land surrounded by mountains

Plain - a big open area of flat land

Plateau - an area of high flat land often with one or more very steep sides or cliffs

River - a natural stream of water flowing into a lake or ocean

Valley - low land lying between hills or mountains

Chapter 2
Geography of Colorado

The bell rang. Mr. Brown's class began to settle into their seats. "It's time for Colorado history. Please take out your atlas," he said. "Let's all point to the state of Colorado." Everyone quickly pointed to the right place. "Good! It's pretty easy to show someone where Colorado is on a map. Now, let's all close our atlases. If you didn't have a map, do you think you could tell someone exactly where to find Colorado?"

Adam raised his hand immediately. "That's easy," he said. "It is almost in the center of the United States."

"That's right," said Mr. Brown. "Can anyone tell me which states surround Colorado?"

"Wyoming and Nebraska are north of Colorado," said Maria.

"Actually, part of Nebraska is north of Colorado and part of it is east," stated Mr. Brown.

"I know that when we drive west we go into Utah and when we drive east we go into Kansas," added Gania.

"That's right, we can say that Utah is to the west of Colorado and Kansas is to the east," said Mr. Brown. "Does anyone know which states are south of Colorado?"

"Oklahoma and New Mexico," said Joe. "Last summer we went to a place called *Four Corners*. You could stand in this special spot. When you put your feet and hands on the marks, you could be in four states at the same time. It was really neat."

Colorado has 7 neighbors.

"Good for you, Joe," said Mr. Brown. "Did you know that Four Corners is the only place in the United States where you can stand in four states at one time? Can you tell us what the four states are, Joe?"

23

"Colorado, New Mexico and Utah are three of them," said Joe. "I can't remember the other one."

"I think it is Arizona," said Abigail. "I got to stand in that spot when we were on a trip two summers ago."

"You have done a really good job of telling about Colorado's neighbors," Mr. Brown smiled. "Now, who thinks they can tell me exactly where Colorado is located?"

Kate raised her hand. "Wyoming and part of Nebraska are north of Colorado, the other part of Nebraska and Kansas are east, Oklahoma and New Mexico are south and Utah is west. At Four Corners, a tip of Arizona touches Colorado."

"Great," said Mr. Brown. "Who can tell us more about Four Corners?"

Chelsea raised her hand and Mr. Brown called on her. "Four Corners is in the southwest corner of Colorado. This is the spot where four states meet. They are Colorado, New Mexico, Arizona and Utah," she said.

"I think you could all do a good job of telling someone just where Colorado is. Can anyone tell me anything else about Colorado?"

"Colorado isn't as big as Texas, but it is a big state," said Abigail.

"That's right, Colorado is the 8th largest state in the U.S. It has 104,100

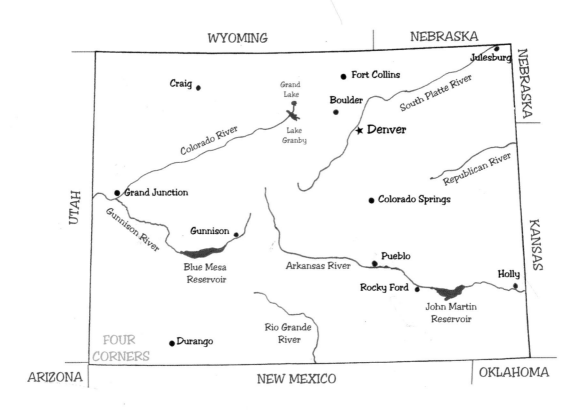

square miles inside its borders. Sometimes it is easier to understand how big something really is if you compare it to a familiar thing. I think that most of you know how large a football field is. You could fit 640 football fields side by side and end to end in one square mile. That means you could fit more than 66 million football fields inside the borders of Colorado."

"Wow! That's a lot of football fields," exclaimed Kelsey.

"It sure is. As a matter of fact, if we could use a giant rolling pin and flatten out the many mountains in Colorado, our state would be even bigger than Texas. Only the state of Alaska would be larger," Mr. Brown told the class.

"Why is Colorado the shape it is?" asked Yeong Se. "It looks like someone took a ruler and drew the borders."

"That is a really interesting point, Yeong Se," said Mr. Brown. "Let's talk a little about how borders are made. Some borders are drawn along special straight lines called **longitude** and **latitude**. You can see these special lines drawn on a map or a globe. They are not drawn on the earth. They are really imaginary lines. The north and south borders of Colorado are drawn on latitude lines. The western and eastern borders are drawn on longitude lines."

"How come all the states don't have nice straight borders like Colorado?" asked Bryan.

"The borders of some states are formed by natural **landforms** such as rivers or mountains. For example, look on your maps at the border between Idaho and Montana. That is really crooked because it is drawn along the top of a mountain range. On the other side of Idaho you will see another crooked border. That is formed by a river.

"Some state borders, like those in Colorado, are formed along lines of latitude and longitude. Other state borders are formed by natural landforms.

"All of the things we have been talking about are part of the geography of Colorado. When we study geography we look at three different things. We learn about **elevation**, **climate**, and landforms."

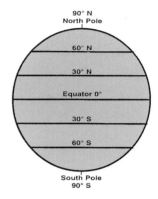

Latitude lines go east and west.

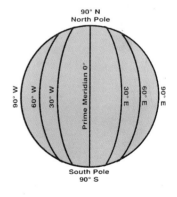

Longitude lines go north and south.

Elevation

"Let's talk about elevation first," said Mr. Brown.

"What do you mean by elevation?" asked Zach.

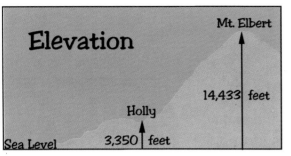

Elevation tells us how high or low the land is compared to sea level.

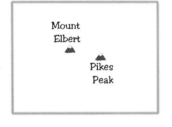

"Elevation tells us how high or low the land is. It is measured in feet above or below sea level. The top of the ocean is at 0 feet. The top of a mountain may be 14,000 feet. That means that the mountain rises 14,000 feet above the level of the ocean. When you climb a 14,000 foot mountain, it does not mean that you go up 14,000 feet from where you started. For example, *Pikes Peak*, is 14,110 feet high, but you climb only 7,540 feet to get to the top. The reason is because Pikes Peak is already on high ground. The ground around Pikes Peak is 6,570 feet above sea level.

"Speaking of sea level, did you know that some scientists believe that much of Colorado was once covered by the ocean? This was millions of years ago before the tall Rocky Mountains were formed. Earthquakes, volcanoes, and glaciers all played a part in shaping our land. The tall southern Rocky Mountains are among the youngest mountains in our country.

"Does anyone know what the highest spot in Colorado is?" asked Mr. Brown.

"Is it Pikes Peak?" asked Jessie.

Mount Elbert is the highest peak in Colorado.
(Credit: C.H.S.)

"Pikes Peak is pretty tall, but it isn't the highest," said Mr. Brown. "Colorado has more than fifty 'fourteeners' or peaks that are over 14,000 feet high. The tallest is *Mt. Elbert*. It is 14,433 feet high. That is almost 2 ¾ miles above sea level. Mt. Elbert is the 19th highest peak in the United States. There are also more than a thousand peaks in Colorado that are over 10,000 feet high."

"My grandpa and grandma live near **Leadville**. You can see Mt. Elbert out of their window," said Nicole. "My grandpa thinks **Mt. Massive** looks higher than Mt. Elbert."

"I've heard that some people think that is true," said Mr. Brown. "I know that they have measured very carefully and found that Mt. Elbert is really 12 feet higher than Mt. Massive. That is not a lot, but it does make Mt. Elbert the highest mountain in Colorado.

The lowest point in Colorado is 3,350 feet on the Arkansas River near the town of Holly.
(Credit: C.H.S.)

"Colorado is the highest state, or has the highest average elevation, in the United States. The average elevation is 6,800 feet. That is more than a mile high. I am sure you have all heard **Denver** called the '**Mile High City**.' That is because Denver's elevation is 5,280 feet, which is one mile above sea level. There is a special marker on the steps of the capitol in Denver that is exactly one mile high. The lowest place in Colorado is near the town of **Holly** where the **Arkansas River** flows at 3,350 feet.

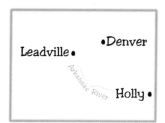

"It is much cooler at the top of a mountain than it is at the bottom. It is about 3° cooler for every 1,000 feet you go up. When it is 70° at 7000 feet then it will be about 49° at the top of a 14,000 foot mountain. After 11,000 feet you come to an area that is above the **treeline**."

"What do you mean by treeline?" asked Bryan.

"It is the elevation above which trees just can't grow. This area is called **alpine tundra**. The growing period for any plant may be only 5 or 6 weeks long. Cold winds often blow at that altitude. Much of the alpine tundra looks like it is just bare rock, but there are many small plants and grasses that grow here. People almost have to get down on their hands and knees to see and appreciate the beauty of the plants that grow high up on the mountain tops. Many of the rocks are partly covered with lichens and mosses. There are also several kinds of insects, birds, and mammals that live in this area."

Alpine tundra is a rocky wind swept area. Patches of snow may still be found in this area even in July.

27

• Gunnison

The LaVeta Hotel around 1902.
(Credit: C.H.S.)

The free meal offer was
written on this old clock.
(Credit: C.H.S.)

"Climate is another part of geography. The climate is the type of weather usually found in an area. For example, when you think of Hawaii, what kind of weather would you expect?" asked Mr. Brown.

"It's always warm and sunny in Hawaii," said Erin. "I've seen lots of pictures of it."

"Well, my mom and dad went there last year. They said that it rained a lot of the time they were there," stated Keith.

"You are both right," said Mr. Brown. "Hawaii is usually warm and sunny, but there are times when it is rainy and cool. The average climate in Colorado is very different from the average climate in Hawaii. Colorado as a whole has a dry, cool, and sunny climate. The state of Colorado has an average of 296 sunny days a year.

"The old LaVeta Hotel in **Gunnison** first opened its doors in April of 1884. At one time they had a very unusual way of advertising. They said that any day the sun did not shine the people staying at the hotel could have a free meal. On July 18, 1935 the records from the LaVeta showed that there had been only 16 days without sun in the past 23 years.

"The climate in the mountains of Colorado is different from the climate on the eastern plains. The mountains, on the western slope of Colorado, get a lot more **precipitation** than the eastern plains. Precipitation is rain, snow, or any other kind of moisture that falls from the sky. The western slope gets as much as 60 inches of precipitation each year. Much of this is snow in the mountains. The eastern plains get only about 16 inches or less."

"Why would the western part of the state get so much more precipitation?" asked Paul.

"The clouds that blow into Colorado from the west and sometimes from the north are stopped by the high Rocky Mountains. The clouds then rise so they can get over the mountains. As they rise the moisture gets cooler and drops out of the clouds. By the time these same clouds get

28

over the mountains and to the plains, they have already lost most of their moisture," said Mr. Brown.

"How come most of the farms in Colorado are on the eastern plains?" asked Kevin. "It would be pretty hard to farm without much water wouldn't it?"

"Good question, Kevin. **Irrigation** is the reason there are so many farms on the plains of eastern Colorado. Does anyone know what irrigation is?" asked Mr. Brown.

"My uncle has a farm near *Rocky Ford*. He raises cantaloupe and I know that he has to use irrigation to get enough water to the cantaloupe plants. He told me he couldn't grow his cantaloupe without irrigation water," said Juan.

"Good job, Juan," praised Mr. Brown. "Farmers use different ways of getting water to their crops. Whenever they bring water to their fields from somewhere else, it is called irrigation. The plains area would be too dry for farming if it were not for irrigation."

Irrigation makes farming possible in many parts of Colorado.

Rocky Ford •

Landforms

"Another important part of geography is the shape of the land," continued Mr. Brown. "Can anyone name one of the landforms found in Colorado?"

"Aren't **mountains** a landform?" asked Kelli. "Colorado sure has a lot of those."

"Yes," said Mr. Brown. "Mountains are an important landform found in Colorado. We have many different landforms. **Valleys**, **plateaus**, **parks**, **plains**, **rivers** and **lakes** are also landforms. Let's begin by talking about mountains."

Mountains

"Mountains have played an important part in the history of Colorado," Mr. Brown said. "The high mountains often made things difficult for the early explorers, mountain men and

miners. Even today when someone wants to go from eastern Colorado to western Colorado a high mountain pass must be crossed. Usually in the summer it is fine, but in the winter it can become a big problem. Can anyone tell me about a mountain in Colorado that they know about?"

Katharine Lee Bates wrote "America the Beautiful" after her visit to the top of Pikes Peak.
(Credit: C.H.S.)

"My dad climbed Pikes Peak when he was in college. I think it was some kind of race that they have every year," said Michael. "He said that it was really a hard race."

"Lots of people have found out that climbing Pikes Peak isn't very easy," said Mr. Brown.

"Didn't you say there was a train that runs to the top of Pikes Peak?" asked Lindsay.

"Yes, in 1891, a cog railroad was completed," said Mr. Brown. "My family and I had a great time riding on it this summer. Before there was a railroad, people traveled to the top in wagons. These wagons were pulled by horses. About halfway up there was a place where the horses were unhitched and mules pulled the wagons the rest of the way up. Even after the railroad was completed many people still liked to travel to the top in wagons."

The cog railroad made travel to the top of Pikes Peak easier.
(Credit: C.H.S.)

"I thought I heard something about a song being written on the top of Pikes Peak," said Tim.

"In 1893, a lady named **Katharine Lee Bates** journeyed to the top of Pikes Peak in one of those wagons. From the top she could see the country spread out before her. She was so inspired by the beauty of what she saw that she later wrote the words to the song, 'America the Beautiful'," said Mr. Brown.

"Does anyone know anything else about our mountains?"

"I know that we have more

Many people made the trip to the top of Pikes Peak by wagon.
(Credit: C.H.S.)

'fourteeners' than any other state," said Yeong Se.

"Good listening, Yeong Se. More than two thirds of the mountains in the United States over 14,000 feet high are found in Colorado. You may have heard Colorado called the 'rooftop of the nation.' This is because of the high average elevation and the many tall mountains found here.

Halfway House was a good stopping point for travelers heading to the top of Pikes Peak.
(Credit: C.H.S.)

"One of the main mountain ranges found in Colorado is called the *Front Range*. This is part of the Rocky Mountain chain. It runs north and south through Colorado. *Denver* and *Colorado Springs* are two of the cities that lie in the foothills of the Front Range. Actually there are 17 different mountain ranges in Colorado. Does anyone know the name of another range?"

"We went hiking in the *Sangre de Cristo Range* last summer," said Michael. "My dad said that eight of the mountains there were over 14,000 feet."

"That is interesting," said Mr. Brown. "The Sangre de Cristo Range runs north and south through the southern part of Colorado and into the northern part of New Mexico. Together the Front Range and the Sangre de Cristo Ranges form an almost unbroken wall that runs through the middle of the state."

"Where did the name Sangre de Cristo come from?" asked Ed.

"There is a story about a Spanish explorer named *Valverde.* He was traveling towards the mountains before sunrise. When the sun came up over the snow capped mountains the peaks turned a deep red. Valverde cried out, 'Sangre de Cristo!' which means 'blood of Christ.' The mountains have been called the Sangre de Cristos ever since.

"The *San Juan Mountains* are in the southwest part of Colorado. They run from the northwest toward the southeast,"

• Denver

Colorado •
Springs

The San Juan
Mountains tower
over Montrose.

said Mr. Brown as he pointed to the map. "The **Sawatch Range**, just west of the Front Range in the middle of the state, has the largest number of tall mountains of any range in Colorado. This range runs north and south. The **Park Range** in the northern part of Colorado also runs north and south. These ranges we have talked about so far are the five major mountain ranges in Colorado.

"There are twelve smaller ranges. The one near **Grand Junction** is called the **Bookcliff Mountains** and runs for about 190 miles. Does anyone know why this range is called the Bookcliff Mountains?"

• Grand Junction

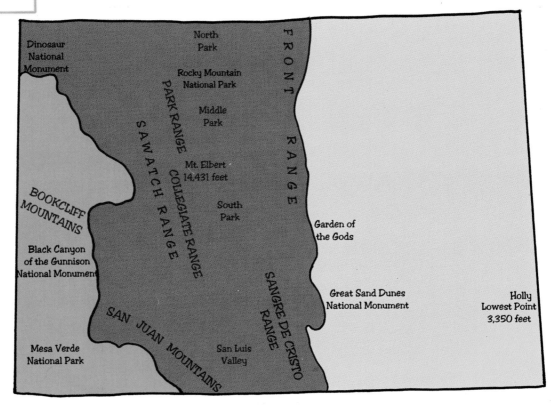

Colorado Plateau
Region

Rocky Mountain
Region

Great Plains
Region

"They look like giant books that have been set up in a bookcase," said Kelli.

"You're right," said Mr. Brown.

"I know that there is a mountain named Harvard," said Tim. "That's where my dad went to college."

"Yes, that mountain is in a special range called the **Collegiate Range**. It also includes mountains named Columbia, Princeton, and Yale," said Mr. Brown.

"Do you know of any other special mountains?"

The Mount of the Holy Cross is in Eagle County.
(Credit: C.H.S.)

"There is a special mountain near the Vail Ski Area. It is called **Mount of the Holy Cross**," said Maria. "We saw it when we went to see my aunt last spring."

"The Mount of the Holy Cross has a deep cut, or **fissure**, in it," said Mr. Brown. "The fissure is about 1,200 feet long and runs up the side of the mountain. Near the top of this fissure is another cut which runs across the mountain. These two cuts form a cross. In the spring when most of the snow has melted there is still a lot of snow in these cracks. You can see an almost perfect white cross.

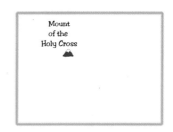

"There is a **legend** that says this mountain was named by some early Spanish explorers. The Mount of the Holy Cross actually became famous in 1876. **William H. Jackson's** photograph of this mountain won a medal in a contest. An artist, **Thomas Moran,** also painted several pictures of this mountain. **Henry Wadsworth Longfellow** wrote a poem called 'The Cross in the Snow' after he saw one of Moran's paintings.

"On top of some of these mountains, that run from north to south through Colorado, there is an imaginary line. Does anyone know what it is called?"

"That's the **Continental Divide,**" said Michael. "My dad explained it to me when we were going over **Monarch Pass** a few weeks ago."

This sign marks the Continental Divide on Monarch Pass.

33

Steep cliffs rise above the Gunnison River in the Black Canyon area.

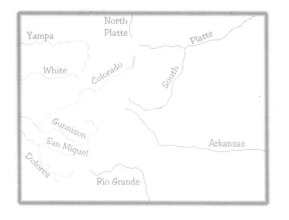

"Can you tell us about it?" asked Mr. Brown.

"Sure. It is an imaginary line that runs along the highest point of the mountains. All the rivers on the west side of the divide run toward the Pacific Ocean and the rivers on the east side run toward the Atlantic."

"Good explanation!" said Mr. Brown.

Rivers

"The Continental Divide is important to Colorado since so many rivers begin in our mountains," Mr. Brown said. "The first river most of us probably think about is the one our state is named after. The *Colorado River* begins at *Grand Lake* in *Rocky Mountain National Park*. It starts out as only a small stream. At 1,450 miles, it is the longest river in the west.

"The Colorado River got its name from some Spanish explorers who saw it at flood stage in 1604. The swift running river carried a lot of silt which gave it a reddish brown color. They named it 'Rio Colorado' which means red river. When the ice and snow from the Rocky Mountains melt, most of this water flows into the Colorado River.

"Many of the rivers that begin in Colorado on the western slope are **tributaries** of the Colorado River."

"What are tributaries?" asked Paul.

"A tributary is a smaller river that flows into a larger one. For example, the *Yampa, White, Gunnison, San Miguel,* and *Dolores* rivers all flow into the Colorado River.

"The Colorado River flows through seven states. It has carved some very special **canyons**. Can anyone tell us a canyon carved by this great river?"

"The Grand Canyon, in Arizona," said Abigail. "When you stand at the top of the canyon, you can hardly see the river at the bottom."

"You're right," said Mr. Brown. "Another canyon is cut by the Gunnison River before it flows into the Colorado River," added Mr. Brown. "It is called the *Black Canyon of the Gunnison*. This canyon is about 50 miles long and the steep cliff walls sometimes rise as much as 3,000 feet above the river. The canyon is about 1,300 feet wide. One of the prettiest sections of this canyon has been made into the **Black Canyon of the Gunnison National Monument**. Does anyone know about another river that begins in Colorado?"

"The **Rio Grande River** begins in Colorado," said Maria.

"Yes, it begins in the San Juan Mountains. It flows to the east for a short distance and then turns south to flow through New Mexico. It forms the border between Texas and Mexico. Is there another river that you think begins in Colorado?" he asked.

"Does the **Platte River** begin in Colorado?" asked Brink.

"Yes it does," answered Mr. Brown. "Both the **North Platte** and the **South Platte** begin in the northern mountains of Colorado. The North Platte flows north into Wyoming, then turns east and goes into Nebraska. The South Platte begins near the middle of the state. It flows northeast into Nebraska where the two rivers meet to form the Platte River."

"My family took a raft trip down the **Arkansas River**. Does that begin in Colorado?" asked Bryan.

"It sure does," said Mr. Brown. "The Arkansas is a major river that begins in the mountains of central Colorado not too far from Mt. Elbert. It then flows south and east through **Pueblo** and **Lamar** and then on into Kansas. The Arkansas River is a major tributary that empties into the Mississippi River. On its way through Colorado it cuts a very deep canyon. Does anyone know what we call that canyon?"

"It's the **Royal Gorge**," said Keith. "We went there with my cousins one summer. You can walk across the **gorge** on a bridge. My dad didn't like the bridge because it was built in 1929 by an amusement company. He said he didn't trust it. It looked safe to me and lots of people walk on it every day. But it sure is a long way to the bottom from the bridge."

"You are right. It is just over 1,000 feet to the bottom of

The Arkansas River has cut this steep canyon called the Royal Gorge.
(Credit: C.H.S.)

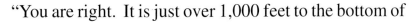

the gorge from the bridge. It looks even further because the cliffs are so steep. The Royal Gorge is part of what is called the '***Grand Canyon of the Arkansas***.'   It is 4 ½ miles long and a railroad runs along the bottom of the gorge. There is also a little cog train that will take you down to the bottom of the gorge.

"There is another major river that begins in Colorado not too far from ***Limon.*** It is the ***Republican River***. It flows northeast into Kansas and then on into Nebraska.

"Colorado is unusual because hardly any rivers flow into Colorado. Most of them start in Colorado and flow into our neighboring states. Our state is sometimes called the '***Mother of Rivers***.' "

Lakes

"Does anyone know where the largest lake in Colorado is?"

"I think it is ***Blue Mesa***" said Adam.

"Blue Mesa **Reservoir** is on the Gunnison River near the town of Gunnison. It has a 27 mile shoreline and is about 9 miles long. It is a beautiful lake and is the largest lake in Colorado, but it is man-made," said Mr. Brown. "Colorado has many man-made lakes called reservoirs. Dams have been built on many rivers creating lakes or reservoirs to store water. These man-made lakes are also used for recreation.

"***Grand Lake*** is the largest natural lake in Colorado. Our state has many other natural lakes high up in the mountains. None of them are very large."

Blue Mesa Reservoir is the largest man-made lake in Colorado.

South Park stretches out to meet the mountains that surround it.

Parks

"Another landform I mentioned earlier is a park," continued Mr. Brown.

"Park? Do you mean a park like City Park?" asked Ed.

"No, the kind of park that we are talking about is a high level meadow between mountain ranges," answered Mr. Brown. "Colorado has four areas that are called parks. The largest of these parks is the *San Luis Valley*. This large flat area is surrounded by the *San Juan*, the *Sangre de Cristo,* and *Sawatch* mountain ranges. The San Luis Valley is a rich agricultural area in the southern part of the state.

"*South Park* is in the central part of the state on the east side of the *Front Range*. It is about 40 miles long. There are many streams and small lakes in this park. When you come down out of the mountains onto this flat valley, you feel like you should be only a few hundred feet above sea level. In fact you are almost 10,000 feet high. There are lots of cattle ranches in South Park.

"The other two parks, *Middle Park* and *North Park,* are on the Western Slope. Middle Park is completely walled by mountains. North Park, in the far north part of the state, is a major ranching area."

Plains

"One of the first landforms the pioneers coming into eastern Colorado saw was the *Great Plains*. The **plains** are an area of flat grassland that stretches across eastern Colorado for hundreds of miles up to the base of the mountains. As the pioneers came through this area, they saw lines of cottonwood and willow trees along the banks of some of the streams. Buffalo and antelope roamed through this area. The grass was only green for a short time in the spring and then it turned brown. In the summer the eastern plains did not look like good farmland. Today, thanks to irrigation, the Great Plains is one of the richest farming areas in the country. Even though the plains look flat, they do slope up towards the mountains. The plains near the mountains are almost 4,000 feet higher than they are near the Colorado and Kansas border."

Plateaus

"A plateau is another landform found in Colorado," said Mr. Brown.

"What is a plateau?" wondered Erin.

"A plateau is an area of high flat land. The **Colorado Plateau**, in the western portion of our state, actually covers parts of four states. Besides Colorado it is in Utah, Arizona and New Mexico. It is much higher than the plains and is much drier than most of the state. The plateau is very rich in minerals such as oil shale and uranium. There are many orchards on the Colorado Plateau. The way the plateau nestles into the mountains helps to hold the heat from the day and keeps the nights warmer. The climate in this area, along with irrigation, makes it possible to raise wonderful fruit."

Unusual Landforms

"Besides all of the landforms we have talked about, we have some unusual landforms here in Colorado. Can anyone think of one?"

"Would the Great Sand Dunes be a landform?" asked Kate.

"Yes, the **Great Sand Dunes National Park** is in south central Colorado. The tallest sand dunes in North America are found there. Some of the dunes are about seven hundred feet high. They lie at the base of the Sangre de Cristo Mountains and run for about 39 miles.

Red Rocks Amphitheater is a natural wonder.

"These dunes were formed when rock was **eroded** by the wind. This created tiny pieces of rock, or sand. This sand was then blown by the strong southwest winds into piles, or dunes.

"Boys and girls love to slide down the dunes on big

sheets of cardboard. Sometimes they ski down on their bare feet."

It is fun to play on the Great Sand Dunes.
(Credit: C.H.S.)

"I know another unusual landform called ***Red Rocks***. It's just outside of Denver," said Lindsay.

"Good," said Mr. Brown. "Red Rocks is what we call a natural **amphitheater**. The rocks are formed just right to make it easy to hear what is happening on the stage. Concerts and programs of many different kinds are held there all summer long.

"The ***Garden of the Gods*** is an area of red rock formations that is found outside of Colorado Springs. There are some beautiful and very unusual formations there. They have been formed by wind and water erosion. Many of the formations have been given special names. Some of my favorites are Sleeping Giant, Balanced Rock, and Kissing Camels.

"We have learned just a few things about Colorado's geography. We have talked about the climate, the elevation and some of the landforms. All of these things had a big influence on our history. Even today, we know that all of these things affect the way people live. On your way home today, see if you can notice any of Colorado's special landforms. Let's put our books away and get ready to go home."

Balanced Rock, at the Garden of the Gods, looks like it is ready to fall.

What Did You Learn?

1. What seven states touch Colorado's borders?
2. What is unusual about the southwest corner of Colorado?
3. What are three main topics we learn about when we study geography?
4. How do we measure elevation?
5. What is the highest point in Colorado? Where is the lowest point?
6. Why does the Western Slope of Colorado get more precipitation than the eastern part of the state?
7. What is a landform?
8. Name three major rivers that begin in Colorado.
9. What gorge in Colorado is sometimes called the "Grand Canyon of the Arkansas?"
10. What is the largest natural lake in Colorado?
11. Tell two interesting facts about South Park.
12. Name two unusual landforms found in Colorado.

What Do You Think?

1. Why do you think Pikes Peak is more famous than Mt. Elbert?
2. If you could visit any place in Colorado, where would you like to go? Why?
3. Why do you think Colorado is sometimes called the "Mother of Rivers?"

Use Your Imagination

1. Imagine you are standing on top of Mount Elbert. How do you feel? What do you think you might see?
2. Make up a story or legend to explain how the Garden of the Gods came to be. Tell how you think the formations got their color?
3. Imagine that you wake up one morning and all the mountains in Colorado are missing. Write a story about what you think it would be like.

Chapter 3
Prehistoric People
of Colorado

"Today in Colorado history, we are going to talk about the first people to come to America," Mr. Brown began.

"You mean the Pilgrims?" asked Michael.

"That is a good guess, but there were many people already here when the Pilgrims came to America less than 400 years ago," said Mr. Brown. "Scientists think that people first came to America at least 15,000 years ago." Mr. Brown pulled down the world map. "It is believed they walked here from the continent of Asia," he said, pointing to the map.

"They couldn't have walked," stated Yeong Se. "There is water between Asia and North America."

"Good point, Yeong Se," said Mr. Brown. "About seventy-five miles of water now separate the two continents. Scientists believe that about 15,000 years ago both North America and Asia were very cold. This cold time was called the **Ice Age.** A large part of both of these continents was covered with ice. It was so cold that the rivers froze. Frozen rivers did not take water back to the ocean. The level of the ocean dropped about 400 feet. This uncovered a stretch of land between the two continents.

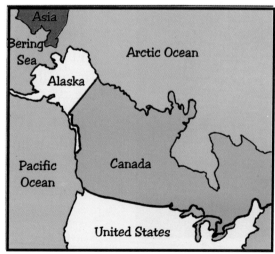

About 75 miles of water now separate Alaska and Asia.

"People walked from Asia in search of food. They began to explore this new land. After a long period of time, they had settled all over North and South America. They developed different **customs** and **cultures** depending on where they lived."

"What do you mean by customs and cultures?" asked Kevin.

Archaeologists find clues about our past buried in the ground.
(Credit: C.H.S.)

"That is the way people live," explained Mr. Brown. "For example, people who settled in cold and snowy areas had a different way of life than people who lived in very warm places. They wore different kinds of clothing and ate different things. They even spoke different languages."

"If they lived that long ago, how do we know how they lived?" asked Brink.

"Great question," praised Mr. Brown. "**Archaeologists** study about people who lived a long time ago. These scientists learn about people by studying the things they have left behind."

The Clovis People

"Archeologists believe that Colorado's earliest people lived here over 12,000 years ago. The *Clovis people* made spear points out of the finest stone. These points were attached to sticks and used for spears. The points were also used like knives to cut up an animal after they killed it.

"The Clovis people also used a tool called the **atlatl**. This was a stick that was used to help them throw their spears with more force. It helped them hunt. The Clovis people hunted big animals like **mammoths.** These animals were so large that one of them could provide enough meat to last a group of people for several months. Some of the meat was dried and some of it was stored in deep pits. The hunters made weapons, shelter, and clothing from the hides of these animals. They used the fat for cooking and to burn in bone lamps.

"It is believed that the early people used the Clovis point until the big game animals like mammoths became **extinct**," continued Mr. Brown.

"Doesn't extinct mean that they all died off?" asked Adam.

"That's correct. Archeologists are not sure why they all died. They could have been hunted to extinction. Another possibility is that the weather changed. After the glaciers from the Ice Age began to disappear, the climate became much drier.

Clovis points were made from fine stone.
(Credit: Denver Museum of Natural History)

Not as much grass grew, so the animals did not have as much to eat. This also could have caused them to die. We do not know for sure. We do know that since the early people were not hunting larger animals any more, they needed to change their spear points. They created smaller and better points. These points became known as ***Folsom Points***."

Folsom People

"Around the year 1900 a black cowboy named **George McJunkin** discovered some old bones. These bones were not like any he had ever seen before. He took them home with him.

"Several years later **J.D. Figgins**, an archeologist, heard about these bones. He found out they were from buffalo that had lived over 10,000 years before. The buffalo were much bigger than those we see today.

"Mr. Figgins went to the area where the bones had been discovered. He found out that at least 30 buffalo had died in this area. As he dug, he also found some spear points.

"The spear points, or large arrowheads, were named after the town of Folsom. They are called Folsom points. The people who lived during that time are now called the ***Folsom people.***

"Over time, Folsom points were found in other areas. One of the most famous of these areas is near ***Fort Collins.*** By studying these areas, archeologists have learned many things about the Folsom people."

"What kinds of things did they find out?" asked Kelli.

"They think that the Folsom people gathered seeds, fruit and nuts from plants. They also hunted animals like deer and buffalo," said Mr. Brown. "Archeologists were able to figure out that the Folsom people used fire."

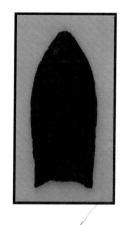

Folsom points were smaller than Clovis points.
(Credit: Denver Museum of Natural History)

Fort Collins •

This painting by Mary Chilton Gray shows Folsom hunters ready to kill a trapped buffalo.
(Credit: Denver Museum of Natural History)

43

"How could they tell that? Did they find old campfires?" questioned Lindsay.

"No, actually, they could tell this by studying old animal bones," answered Mr. Brown. "They could tell that the bones had been cooked, and then split. They also found things such as knives made out of stone, rubbing stones, and tools that were used to scrape animal hides."

"Do they know what the Folsom people looked like?" wondered Maria.

"Archeologists have never found any of the bones of the Folsom people, so they do not know what they looked like," replied Mr. Brown.

Plainview People

This diorama shows hunters trying to kill buffalo.
(Credit: C.H.S.)

"Another group of early Colorado people were the ***Plainview people***. Archeologists do not know how long these people lived in Colorado, or what they looked like. They do know that the Plainview people lived in several different places in eastern Colorado.

"The Plainview people hunted animals like antelope, deer, and buffalo. In one area, archeologists found the skeletons of over 190 buffalo in a large gully near the town of Yuma, Colorado. They believe that the hunters had frightened the buffalo into a gully. The buffalo would trample each other trying to get out. This made it easier for the hunters to kill the buffalo with spears. The spear points that they used were different than the spear points used by the Folsom people."

Basketmaker Period (1-400 AD)

"The Clovis, Folsom, and Plainview people were mostly **nomadic**," began Mr. Brown.

"What does that mean?" asked Abigail.

"Nomadic means that they traveled around a lot. Most of the time they were searching for food. They didn't really have permanent homes.

"Around 1,400 to 2,000 years ago some of them began to settle in caves along the mesas in southwestern Colorado. They began to plant crops like corn. By planting crops, they were not so dependent on hunting for food. This meant they did not have to move around as much.

"They would weave baskets of many sizes, shapes and colors. Because of this, archeologists called them the **Basketmaker culture**. The baskets were woven so tightly, they could hold water. They would use sticky pine pitch to waterproof the baskets. Baskets were used to carry things and also to cook their food."

The Basketmaker people began to settle in caves. *(Credit: C.H.S.)*

"How could you cook in a basket? Wouldn't it burn on a fire?" wondered Nicole.

"Good question," said Mr. Brown. "First they put water and the food in the basket. Hot stones were then dropped into the baskets. This heated the water which would cook the food.

"In the Basketmaker culture, the women cut their hair short. The men allowed theirs to grow long. Some of the men had fancy hairstyles. They often tied their hair in 3 sections. One section would go down each side, and the third section would be worn down the back. Archeologists believe that human hair was sometimes used in their weaving."

Modified Basketmaker Period (400-750 AD)

"Over time, the Basketmakers began to change the way they lived. They started using clay to make pottery. This made it easier to cook and store food. Farming became more developed. They grew beans, squash, and corn of several colors.

"They also began to use bows and arrows, instead of an atlatl, which made it easier to hunt animals. Arrowheads were made of stone or wood. The bows were made from wood and the strings were made of yucca rope or **sinew**. Sinew is the

45

Pit houses gave better protection from the weather.
(Credit: C.H.S.)

This woven sandal was made during the Basketmaker Period.
(Credit: C.H.S.)

tendon or the part of an animal that holds the muscle to the bone.

"The Basketmakers learned to make homes that would give them better protection from the weather. They built **pit houses** inside caves. A pit house was made by digging a pit, or hole, in the ground about 4 feet deep. The sides of the house were made of poles and dried mud. The door was a hole in the flat roof. They would use a ladder to get in and out of their homes."

"Do archeologists know what the Basketmaker people looked like?" asked Zach.

"Archeologists have found the skeletons of people from the Basketmaker culture. The women were only about 5 feet tall and the men were just a little taller. They had brown skin and black hair.

"Not much is known about what they wore. Archeologists have found some yucca aprons that may have been worn by the women. It is believed that the men usually wore a breechcloth, and that the children usually wore nothing. Many sandals woven out of yucca fibers have been found. Blankets and robes were used in the winter to help keep them warm."

Developmental Pueblo Period (750-1100 AD)

"Things changed once again during this period. The people began to group their houses together to form **pueblos**. These were like towns that were built on top of the mesa. These buildings were usually shaped like the letters L, U, or E. Bricks were made of sandstone and were about the size of a loaf of bread. A mixture of mud and water was used to hold the bricks together. The buildings were kind of like apartment houses. They were stacked several stories high. Each family had one room. The room was about 6 feet by 8 feet. It was used for sleeping and storing their things. Some rooms on the upper levels and toward the back were used for storing crops. Nearly all of the houses faced south or southwest."

Houses were grouped together on top of a mesa. *(Credit: C.H.S.)*

"How did they get to the top rooms?" asked Tim.

"There were ladders to connect different floors. They also had shafts, or holes, that would bring in air and let the light in.

"Pottery improved during this time. Different groups made pottery with different designs," continued Mr. Brown. "They also began weaving cotton cloth.

"Cradleboards were used for carrying the babies around. These boards were hard and caused the backs of the babies' heads to become flat in back."

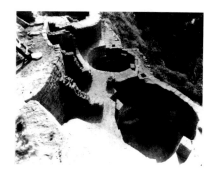

Above: Ruins of a kiva in Mesa Verde. *(Credit: C.H.S.)* Below: The kiva was usually only used by men and boys.

Great or Classic Pueblo Period (1100-1300 AD)

"The next period that archeologists talk about is the Great or Classic Pueblo Period. During this time, the houses were built with stones and held together with adobe mortar. The walls were smoothly plastered and painted with designs of red, yellow, black and white. Their settlements ranged in size from a few rooms to as many as 200 rooms.

"Each building, or group of rooms, had one or more **kivas**. This was a round room that was partially sunk into the ground. These rooms were usually used only by the men and boys for religious ceremonies. Sometimes the medicine men would take sick people into the kiva. The men would also weave in the kivas. They made sleeping blankets and mats on looms.

"In the ground of the kiva was a small hole called a **sipapu**. (see-pah-pu) The Pueblo people believed that all living things came from out of the earth. This hole represented

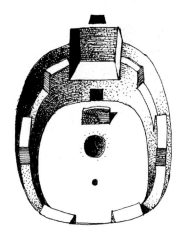

47

Houses were built on a cliff ledge with one house on top of another.
(Credit: C.H.S.)

an entrance from the lower spiritual world.

"By around the year 1200 they began to build their homes on cliff ledges. These ledges stretched back into the cliff like a large open mouthed cave. This gave them more protection from their enemies and the weather. In front of the buildings were large open spaces where the families would gather. They could cook food, work, and play in this area. The ledge overhead would protect them from the sun and the rain.

"The men grew corn, beans, and pumpkins on top of the mesas and in the valleys below. They had to climb stairs or use foot holds to get to their crops. Since this area did not get very much rainfall, they would dam up streams and dig reservoirs to hold water for their crops. Most of their food was grown in the fields. They would also hunt for deer and rabbits. The meat was then stewed or roasted.

"The men also made tools. Axes, scrapers, knives, needles, drills, and awls were made out of wood, stone, and bone. The men did most of the building and wove cloth.

"The women were also very busy. They would clean the rooms and air out the blankets. They would repair their homes, when needed, by putting new plaster on the walls. They

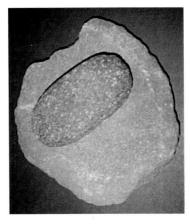

A mano and metate were used to grind corn.

48

would even paint the inside of the rooms. Sometimes they would paint designs or picture stories on their walls.

"The women looked after the children. They prepared the food. Corn was ground using a **mano and metate**. The mano was a round rock that was rubbed over a flat rock called a metate which would crush the food. Berries, nuts, and fruit were also gathered.

"The women used the fiber of the yucca plant for thread to make clothing. They also used yucca fibers to make sandals. Their clothing was decorated with feathers, shells, and colorful stones. They also created beautiful pottery. Jewelry was made out of turquoise and other brightly colored stones."

"Where did they get things like shells?" asked Erin.

"They traded with other Indian tribes. They would take things like deerskins and stone blades to trade for things such as seashells, cotton, salt, and turquoise.

"Spring was a time for marriages. If a girl wanted to marry a boy, she would go to his house. She would squat down and grind corn for four days. If she did a good job, the families would agree on marriage. The boy would make gifts for the girl. The girl's family would build them a house. When it was time, the new couple would move into their house together.

"Very few of these people lived more than 40 years. The winter months were hardest on the oldest and the youngest. Blankets and robes of rabbit fur helped them keep warm during the cold winters. Blankets were sometimes made out of turkey feathers. These were the warmest blankets of all."

"Where did they get turkey feathers?" asked Paul.

"Turkeys were raised by the Pueblo people. The turkeys provided meat, feathers, and bones for tools and jewelry," answered Mr. Brown.

"Did they raise any other animals?" asked Keith.

"They kept dogs as pets," replied Mr. Brown.

Beautiful designs were put on pottery.
(Credit: C.H.S.)

Pottery was made in different shapes.
(Courtesy: National Park Service)

Bows and arrows made hunting easier.
(Courtesy: National Park Service Painting by: Roy Andersen)

Building their homes
under a cliff gave better
protection from the
weather.
*(Courtesy: National Park Service
Painting by Roy Andersen)*

Mesa Verde
National Park

Mesa Verde

"Some of the people we have been learning about settled in the caves at ***Mesa Verde*** in southwest Colorado around 550 A.D. Around 1888, two ranchers, looking for stray cattle, found the Mesa Verde remains. As archeologists studied these people, they began to call them ***Anasazis***. This either means 'ancient ones', 'ancient enemies', or 'ancient ancestors' in the Navajo language. The Anasazis are the ancestors of the modern Pueblo Indians that now live in New Mexico and Arizona. Many Pueblo people do not like the idea that their ancestors have a Navajo name, so they prefer the name ***Ancestral Puebloans***. You will see this group of people called by both of these names. Around 1275-1300 the Mesa Verde people disappeared."

"What happened to them?" asked Gania.

"No one really knows for sure. Most people believe that there was a drought that hit that area around that time. If there was no water for the crops, it would have been difficult to stay in that area. They may have left and gone to the area that is now Arizona and New Mexico."

"How can they tell that there was a drought during that time?" wondered Lindsay.

The men did most of the hunting.
(Courtesy: National Park Service

"Good question," praised Mr. Brown. "Scientists can use tree rings to tell how old a tree is. Each ring represents one year of growth. If the rings were thick, then that was a year when there was a lot of moisture so the tree could grow well. If rings were thinner, then they knew there was not as much moisture during that year.

"Another interesting idea is sometimes used to explain what happened to them. They ground their corn using a mano and metate made from sandstone. Some people believe that pieces of sand from the sandstone would break off into their food. As they ate their food, their teeth would wear down very quickly. By the age of thirty most of them had very little of their teeth remaining. As a result, it was difficult to eat and this caused bad health. This could have been another reason why they disappeared."

"Could they have been killed in a battle with some of their enemies?" wondered Paul.

"There is no evidence of enemies, but we may never really know for sure," answered Mr. Brown.

"I went to Mesa Verde on our trip to Arizona last August," remembered Bryan. "It was awesome."

"I have been there also, and it is one of the neatest things I have ever seen," agreed Mr. Brown. "If any of you get a chance, you should visit Mesa Verde.

"Well, we had better quit for the day. Tomorrow, we are going to talk about the American Indians that were in the Colorado area when the European explorers began to come to this area," concluded Mr. Brown.

Finding enough food was a constant struggle.
(Courtesy: National Park Service
Painting by Roy Andersen)

What Did You Learn?

1. What does an archeologist do?
2. Who do archeologists believe were the first people to live in Colorado?
3. What is the name of the prehistoric spear points found near Fort Collins?
4. How do archeologists think that the Plainview people hunted buffalo?
5. Why were most of the early people in Colorado nomadic?
6. What was the name of the round room in which religious ceremonies of the cliff dwellers took place?
7. Why did the people from the Great or Classic Pueblo period begin to build their homes on cliff ledges?
8. What unusual thing did the Pueblo people use to make blankets?
9. What is one reason archeologists believe the Anasazi or the Ancestral Puebloans left Mesa Verde?
10. Describe a mano and metate and tell how they are used.

What Do You Think?

1. What do you think happened to the people who lived at Mesa Verde around 1275 A.D.? Tell why you believe this way.
2. Would you have liked to live back in the times of the Clovis people? Why or why not?

Use Your Imagination

1. Write a story about what you think a day in the life of a child living in Mesa Verde around 1100 A.D. was like.
2. Imagine you are an archeologist in the year 2795 A.D. You have just discovered the ruins of an elementary school from the year 2000. Write about what you have found and tell what you might learn from these things.

"Yesterday we talked about people who lived in Colorado thousands of years ago. By the time Europeans came to Colorado, there were three main groups of American Indians living in this area. They were the **Utes, Arapaho,** and the **Cheyenne**," said Mr. Brown.

"Today we will begin studying about these different tribes. You will see that in some ways these groups are different. You will also find that many things in their lifestyles are similar. Can anyone guess a way in which they may have been alike?"

Hunting and Gathering Food

"They all hunted for food, didn't they?" suggested Tim.

"Yes. Early tribes spent most of their time gathering and preparing food for their families. The men would do most of the hunting. They used tools like bows and arrows. Until they began trading with other tribes, they did not have metal. They made their tools from stone, wood, and bones," explained Mr. Brown.

"Did they hunt buffalo?" asked Joe.

"Yes," replied Mr. Brown. "Hunting for buffalo was usually a group effort. Before they had horses, they might ambush the buffalo near a water hole. Or they might surround the buffalo on three sides as the animals were grazing. Then they would slowly move in around the herd. The buffalo could not escape on the fourth side, because there would be an **arroyo**, which is like a gully. At the right time, the hunters would come out of hiding and

The bow and arrow were used for hunting.
(Credit: C.H.S.)

53

Sometimes buffalo
would be frightened
into an arroyo.
(Credit: C.H.S.)

shout and yell and wave blankets to scare the buffalo into the arroyo. By the time the buffalo in the front saw the arroyo, it was too late to stop. They were pushed in by the buffalo from behind. The hunters would take the best meat. They ate some of it raw, and took the rest back to camp.

"Once the Indians started using horses, methods of hunting changed. They would slowly get as close to the herd as they could. Then, when the herd saw them and tried to run, the men would chase after them on their fastest horses. This was very dangerous because the horses and the buffalo would be traveling very fast. If a horse were to stumble or a buffalo were to turn the wrong way, it could be deadly. These buffalo hunts would usually provide enough meat to last through the winter."

"What happened to all of the meat? They didn't have any refrigerators," stated Abigail.

"It was hard to keep the meat from spoiling. Sometimes they dried the meat in strips to make **jerky**. They also made **pemmican**. This was made by grinding dried meat into a fine powder. It was then mixed with melted fat from the animal and made into little cakes. Sometimes berries were added to the pemmican."

"Yuck! I'd rather have a peanut butter and jelly sandwich," said Kelsey.

54

"They didn't have peanut butter and jelly sandwiches," said Mr. Brown. "But I'm sure the pemmican tasted good to them."

"I've heard that the Indians would kill an animal only when they needed food," said Chelsea.

The mano was rubbed over the metate to grind roots and other foods.
(Credit: C.H.S.)

"It is true that the Indians respected nature," remarked Mr. Brown. "They usually only took from the land what they needed to survive. They had a use for every part of any animal they killed. Bones were used for tools. The hides were used as tipi coverings and for clothing.

"The women would tan buffalo hides. First, the hides were scraped to remove all of the fat, meat, and sometimes the hair. The hair was left on the hide for tipi coverings. This would help the tipi to stay warmer. For clothing, the hair would be removed. Then the hide was rubbed with a combination of animal brains and soapweed. The hides would be cleaned and then dried in the sun. Finally, the hide was softened by being pulled over a thick rope made of buffalo **sinew**.

"The women also hauled wood and water to the campsite. They gathered nuts and berries, dug roots, and did the cooking. The women would use a **mano and metate** to grind roots into a fine powder. This powder was used for food."

Indian Homes

"How else do you think the different tribes were alike?" continued Mr. Brown.

"They all lived in **tipis**," said Zach.

"The Indians lived in several kinds of shelters. The most common was the tipi. This was a type of tent shaped like an upside down ice cream cone. Poles from lodgepole pine trees were used as a base for the tipi. The poles were covered with buffalo hides. It would take about 10 hides to make a small tipi and as many as 20 hides to make a larger one. Many times the tipis were set up in a semi circle with their doors facing east toward the rising sun.

The tipi was the most common Indian shelter.
(Credit: C.H.S.)

The wickiup was covered with brush and branches.
(Credit: C.H.S.)

"A shelter used by the Ute Indians was the **wickiup.** A wickiup was sometimes built like a lean-to against a tree. It had straight sides. It was covered with branches and brush. At times stones were put around the bottom to keep the poles stable. Some wickiups were built in the shape of a tipi. Not all wickiups were used as homes. Sometimes they were used as war lodges. Once they were made, they were left in place so they could be used by hunters, war parties and travelers.

"During the summers, many of the Indians lived in the mountains where it was cooler," Mr. Brown went on. "During the winter, they would move to the deserts and valleys. These places were warmer and had less snow.

"Most Indians lived in small groups or bands. By living together, they could protect themselves better. The people could also hunt together."

Communication

"You said that most of the tribes had different languages. How could they talk to each other?" asked Brink.

"**Sign language** was one way the Indians talked to one another. They would use their arms and hands to make signs."

"Is that kind of like the sign language we use today with people who cannot speak or hear?" asked Juan.

"It is the same idea," said Mr. Brown. "Rock art was also a way of communicating. It was not a written language. Symbols were painted on rocks to create a **pictograph.** The paint was made by mixing plants and minerals with water,

Petroglyphs were symbols scratched into the rock.
(Credit: C.H.S.)

oil, or grease. The American Indians painted symbols on the rocks with their fingers, strips of animal skin, or pieces of fur.

"Another form of rock art was the **petroglyph.** These were formed by scratching symbols into a rock with a stone. It is hard to find rock art today. Time and weather have worn many of the symbols away."

Transportation

"Being able to communicate was really important to the Indians. Transportation was also important. How do you think they got from place to place?" asked Mr. Brown.

Horses made transportation easier.
(Credit: C.H.S.)

"They walked," said Jessie.

"They walked a lot, but how else did they get around?" asked Mr. Brown.

"They rode horses!" exclaimed Bryan.

"You're right. Horses lived in Colorado long ago, but they all died. There had been no horses in Colorado for a long time. Before the Spanish brought horses with them to Mexico, the Indians had never seen horses before. Horses really changed the lives of most of the tribes. They made hunting easier. The Indians were able to hunt larger animals. Horses became a sign of wealth. They were often sold or given as gifts. Some were stolen during raids on other tribes."

"I've seen pictures of horses pulling long poles behind them," said Kate.

"That is called a **travois,**" said Mr. Brown. "Two long poles tied together were fastened to the horse. The other end of the poles would drag along the ground. They would fasten a skin between the poles. Then they could pile things they wanted to carry on the travois. For a long time, the American Indians had used dogs as pack animals and to pull a small travois. Once they had horses, they found they could carry even larger loads."

The travois was used to carry things behind a horse or a dog.
(Credit: C.H.S.)

57

Indian Children

"Have you ever thought about what it would have been like to be an Indian child living long ago?" asked Mr. Brown.

"I'll bet all they had to do was play. They didn't have to go to school," said Gania. "I think I would like that."

"I don't think it was an easy life," Mr. Brown continued. "Indian children helped their parents with the chores. The boys would help their fathers with the hunting. The girls helped their mothers prepare the food. They also helped take care of the younger children. When the work was finished, they liked to play games and have fun.

"The Indian children did not have televisions, bicycles, or any of the fancy things you have today. They enjoyed dancing, running races, and swimming. Even though they didn't go to school like you do, they were still learning. All of the chores and even the games they played helped to get them ready for the life they lived."

"It sounds like they liked doing many of the same things we like to do," said Nicole.

"You're right. They also liked to listen to stories just like most of you. Their grandparents and parents would share stories called **legends**. These are stories about creation, people, and animals. Legends were often used to explain why certain things happened. These stories continue to help keep American Indian traditions, culture, and history alive."

"I would like to hear some of the stories they told," said Maria.

"Let me tell you a quick Ute legend," said Mr. Brown.

"Almost all of the Indian tribes have a story of creation. This is a story that explains where they believe they came from. I am going to share with you one version of the Ute creation legend.

Children from a southern Ute tribe
(Credit: C.H.S.)

"According to the legend, at one time there were no people in any part of the world. The creator began to cut sticks and place them in a large bag. He continued to do this for some time until Coyote became so curious that one day, he opened the bag. Lots of people came out of the bag. They were all speaking different languages and they began to go in different directions. When the creator came back, only a few people were still there. He was very mad at Coyote. The creator wanted to place the people equally around the land. Now, since the people were scattered unequally, there would be war between them. They would try to get land from each other. There were a few people still in the bag. The creator decided that these people would be the Ute Indians. Even though they would be a small tribe, they would be very brave and be able to defeat all of the other people.

"You may hear this story told in different ways depending on who is telling the story. I hope you enjoyed it. There are some books of legends on the back table if you would like to read one later," encouraged Mr. Brown.

Ute Indians in front of a tipi
(Credit: C.H.S.)

"How would you like to learn more about each of the tribes that lived in Colorado?" asked Mr. Brown. The whole class nodded their heads. "Let's learn some more about the Ute Indians."

The Ute

"The **Ute Indians** lived on the western slope of the Rocky Mountains. They came from Utah around 1500. The Ute Indians call themselves '**Nooch**' or '**Nunche**' which means 'the people.' The word Ute comes from an Indian word '**Eutaw**' or '**Yuta**' that means 'people of the mountains.' The Ute Indian tribe was the largest and oldest tribe living in Colorado when European explorers began to come into Colorado.

"Life was not always easy for the Ute Indians. They were not farmers. They were **nomadic**. The men would hunt animals like buffalo, elk, deer, mountain sheep, and rabbits. They also fished, hunted birds, and

The yucca plant was used for many things.

caught insects to eat."

"You mean they ate insects?" asked Ed surprised.

"Sure. Insects like grasshoppers and crickets are a good source of protein," replied Mr. Brown. "The women would also gather plants and berries to eat. The yucca plant was a very important plant to them. The blossom and the fruit were used to eat. Soap was made out of the root. Fiber from the leaves was used to weave things like sandals. Pinion nuts were also an important part of their diet. In the summer, they would search in the mountains for food. In the winter, they looked in the valleys.

"It was not always easy to find enough to eat, so they often went hungry during the winter months. The tribe would break up into family groups during the winter. This group might include a mother, a father, the children, grandparents, aunts, uncles, and cousins."

"Why did they break up into groups instead of all staying together?" asked Keith.

"It was easier for a smaller group to find enough food than it was for a large group. The grandparents or young girls would take care of the children while the parents searched for food. The babies would be carried on a **cradleboard**. The children were considered very important. They were never spanked and hardly ever punished, but even at a young age they were working hard to help their families survive.

This Ute mother has strapped her baby to a cradleboard.
(Credit: C.H.S.)

"The Utes believed that the older people were the wisest. They were treated with a lot of respect. At mealtimes, the older people would be the first to be served. The others would not take a bite or a drink before the eldest person did. It was also considered bad manners to speak before the eldest person had spoken. The grandfather was also the one who decided when it was time to move on.

"Hunting and gathering food took up a lot of their time, but they still liked to play games. One of the favorite Ute activities was to play a dice game. The dice were made out of

The Bear Dance
celebrates the
beginning of new life
in the spring.
(Credit: C.H.S.)

pieces of willow wood.

"Another game, **<u>Shinny</u>**, was played by teams of 10-25 women using curved sticks. The field was a little shorter than a football field with a goal at each end. The object of the game was to move the ball to the opponent's goal. The ball could be moved by either kicking it or hitting it with the stick."

"It kind of sounds like a combination of hockey and soccer," noticed Erin.

"You're right," laughed Mr. Brown. "The men also liked to play a game like darts. They used a hoop as a target. The hoop was rolled along the ground.

"In the spring the Ute groups would all come back together. They would know it was time to gather when they heard the first spring thunder. This was usually around mid-March. It was time for the annual **<u>Bear Dance</u>**. The Bear Dance symbolized the beginning of new life in the spring. It is said that long ago a Ute hunter saw a bear come out of his winter den and begin to dance. The bear told the hunter that if he would copy the bear's dance, he would become a successful hunter and a better husband. So, every year, the Utes perform the Bear Dance.

"The men prepared the dance corral while the women made festive clothing to wear at the dance. The dance lasted for several days. The women would ask the men to dance. Some of the men would play **<u>moraches</u>**. The morache was a musical instrument that sounds like a bear growling. It is sometimes

A deer shinbone
was rubbed
against the
morache to make
a growling sound.
(Credit: C.H.S.)

61

called a 'bear growler.'

"A cedar tree was planted at the east entrance of the dance corral. At the close of the dance, they would leave eagle feathers, that they had worn, on the tree. When these feathers would blow in the breeze, this represented leaving behind all of the troubles of the past. It was a new beginning.

"The Utes dressed in plain buckskin clothing until they began to have contact with the Plains Indians. Then they started to decorate their clothing with beads and porcupine quills.

"The men wore deerskin breechcloths, deerskin leggings, and moccasins. They wore deerskin shirts when needed.

"The women wore skirts made of buckskins or woven with bark and reeds. The skirts were knee length. Deerskin leggings, that came up to just below the knee, were also worn.

"The Utes liked to wear jewelry. They often wore small polished bones in their noses. Necklaces were made out of animal claws, bone beads, stones, and seeds. Fancy belts were sometimes worn.

Ute Indian dress
(Credit: C.H.S.)

"On special occasions, they painted their faces. Sometimes they tattooed their faces. They would pierce their skin with the sharp point of a cactus. The thorns would be dipped in a mixture of water and ashes. The color of the ashes would stay in the scar creating a tattoo. Sometimes they decorated their hair with white and black paint and feathers.

"The Ute winter hunting grounds were close to some towns in northern Mexico. The Ute Indians were amazed when they saw horses in these towns. They knew that horses would be a great thing to have.

"The Ute Indians began to trade with the Spanish and other Indians for horses. They did not have money, gold, or silver. The only thing they had to trade was meat or animal hides. Since they usually only had enough food for their own

62

families, they needed to think of another way to get horses.

"The Spanish needed children to take care of their animals, and to help clean their houses, so Ute children were sometimes traded or even kidnapped to work on the Spanish ranches. The children learned many things about horses. Once they had learned how to care for horses, sometimes they would steal some of the horses and return to their own homes.

"The Comanche Indians who lived south of the Utes had a lot of horses. Many times the Utes would steal the Comanche horses. This made the two tribes bitter enemies. Sometimes they raided other tribes. The Ute Indians became a strong tribe that was feared by other tribes."

The Plains Indians

"There were several tribes that lived in the plains of eastern Colorado. The *Arapaho* were the first to move west to the plains. They had been forced off their land by other Indian tribes. They had been farmers, but had to change their lifestyle to live in the plains. They began to hunt buffalo, deer, rabbits, and other animals. They also gathered nuts and berries.

"The name Arapaho may have come from the Crow Indian word '*Alappaaho*' which means 'People With Many Tattoos'. Many Arapaho men had tattoos of three small circles across their chests. Many women had a tattoo on their forehead.

"The Arapaho women wore dresses that hung almost to the ankle. Their moccasins had leggings attached that covered the lower part of their legs. The men wore buckskin shirts, breechcloths, and moccasins. Leggings that covered them from ankle to hip were worn. In the winter, blankets and buffalo robes were used to keep warm.

"An Arapaho family usually included a man, his wife or wives, their children, and sometimes another relative. Many men had two wives. The wealthier a man was, the more wives he usually had. Each family had its own tipi.

"Most marriages were arranged by a young girl's father, brother, or uncle. The bride's family would usually set up a tipi for the young couple. Then they would invite the groom and his family there for a feast. The elders would pray for the young people and tell them how to live as a married couple. The two families would give each other gifts.

"The **Cheyenne** also moved to the plains. Before they moved, they had been farmers and lived in houses made out of sticks and covered with mud. They were forced off their land by the Sioux Indians. They became nomads who hunted and gathered their food.

"The Cheyenne called themselves '*Tsistsistas*'. This means 'the beautiful people'. The Cheyenne Indians became one of the most feared and admired Indian tribes in the 1800s.

"The Cheyenne women wore loose deerskin dresses that reached below the knee. The men wore breechcloths. In cold weather, the men also wore leggings. Both men and women used buffalo robes to keep warm in winter. Many times these robes were decorated with small beads and porcupine quills.

"Women who made 30 or more pieces of clothing and were really good at doing porcupine quillwork could become members of the **Robe Quillers Society**. This was a high honor for a woman. The women of this group were respected just like men who had become warriors.

"It was not polite for a young man to ask a woman to marry him. One of his relatives, usually an elderly female, would go to the family to ask. If the family of the boy was happy with the girl he had chosen, they would give the girl's family many gifts. If the girl's family decided against the marriage, the gifts would be returned. If the families approved of the marriage, the girl was carried by the groom's relatives and friends into the tipi of the groom's family. She was set in a place of honor. The bride's new female relatives would dress her in fancy clothes for the special day. They would redo her hair and paint her face. Finally there would be a big feast. Soon after, the new couple would move into their own tipi.

"A Cheyenne family might include an older couple, their unmarried children, plus their married daughters and families.

"The Cheyenne and the Arapaho were friends. Sometimes they joined together to make war or to hunt.

"Some other tribes sometimes lived in the plains of eastern Colorado. They were the **Pawnee, Comanches, Kiowas, Apaches, Crows, Navajos**, and the **Sioux**. The Sioux were sometimes called **Dakota, Lakota**, or **Nakota.**

Just then the bell for recess rang. "Oh, I guess we are

out of time. I hope you all learned some things about the American Indians of Colorado. As we study more this year, we will learn about the problems between the settlers and the Indians. We will also learn about the American Indians who are living in Colorado today.

"Let's get cleaned up and go outside for recess."

What Did You Learn?

1. Why did the Indians make jerky?
2. How was pemmican made?
3. Describe how the Indians made buffalo hides soft.
4. What was the most common home used by the Indians of Colorado?
5. Describe the difference between a petroglyph and a pictograph.
6. How did horses change the way of life for the Indians?
7. Describe a travois. Tell how it was used.
8. What are three ways the yucca plant was used by the Indians?
9. When European explorers first came into Colorado, which tribe was the largest and had lived in Colorado the longest?
10. What did women have to do to become members of the Robe Quillers Society?

What Do You Think?

1. What do you think it would have been like to be an Indian child before the settlers came? How would your life change after their arrival?
2. The American Indians tried very hard not to waste things. How do you think our world would be different if we all lived like that?
3. What do you think the Indian girls liked to do best? Why?
4. What do you think the Indian boys liked to do best? Why?

Use Your Imagination

1. Imagine you are an Indian. You have just received your own horse. Describe your horse. Tell what you would do and where you would go.
2. Read some Indian legends. Now write a legend of your own.

Chapter 5
Exploration of Colorado

The students in Mr. Brown's class were just finishing their math lesson for the day. "When you are finished with your assignment, I would like you to write in your journals for a little while," instructed Mr. Brown.

"Yuck! I don't like writing in my journal!" exclaimed Zach. "A journal is just like a diary, and diaries are for girls!"

"Well, Zach, it is a good thing that many people, including men, have kept journals. If explorers like *Zebulon Pike* and *Stephen Long* had not kept journals, we would not know about their early journeys into Colorado. In fact, several explorers from Europe may have come to Colorado between 1541 and 1694, but we do not know for sure. There are no records to prove it because they didn't keep journals.

"Some people think that a man named *Coronado* may have actually been the first European to come to Colorado. He was searching for gold. This was in 1541, which is less than 50 years after Columbus made his first trip to the new world. Coronado probably didn't come this far northwest. We really wish he had kept a journal so we would know.

"Some of the early explorers stayed and settled in what is now New Mexico. One of these early Spaniards did keep a journal. In 1694, *Diego de Vargas* was chasing some Indians. They were slaves who had run away. He came into what is now Colorado. His is the first

This painting by Frederic Remington shows Coronado's march.
(Credit: C.H.S.)

written record of Europeans coming into the area that is now Colorado," continued Mr. Brown.

"We also know that *Juan Ulibarri* came into Colorado in 1706, because he kept a written record. He discovered the *Arkansas River*. One of the areas where he camped was near what is now the city of *Pueblo*. He discovered that French trappers had been in this area. He was afraid that the French were going to claim this land, so Ulibarri claimed it for Spain."

"What do you mean he claimed the land for Spain?" asked Lindsay.

"To claim something is to say that it belongs to you. Since Spain was the first European country to explore this area, they felt they had the right to claim this land for Spain," explained Mr. Brown.

"What about the Indians?" asked Brink. "They lived in this area first. Wouldn't the land belong to them?"

"Good point, Brink. That would make sense, but many of the Europeans did not care about the Indians or their rights," responded Mr. Brown.

"At one time Spain claimed much of the western and the southeastern parts of what is now our state," answered Mr. Brown. "Spain wasn't the only European nation that wanted to own this land. In 1682, a French explorer named *LaSalle* traveled down the Mississippi River. He claimed all of the Mississippi River and all the land that drained into the river for France. This would include all of the eastern slope of Colorado. France and Spain had claimed some of the same land.

"Spain really wanted to keep this area. In 1720, they sent *Pedro de Villasur* into southeastern Colorado. He was supposed to drive the French out, but he was killed by Indians.

"One of the main expeditions into Colorado by the Spanish began in Santa Fe on July 29, 1776. *Father Escalante* and *Father Dominguez* with eight other Spaniards set out to find a route to the California missions. They left *Santa Fe* in hopes of building new missions along the way. They went northward through western Colorado to avoid some unfriendly Hopi and Apache tribes. They found and named what is now the *Dolores River*. They also spotted and described the ruins of an ancient Pueblo Indian settlement.

"They then traveled south through Utah. The group ran

into heavy snows and headed back to Santa Fe. Father Escalante kept a journal of their travels. Another member of the group drew maps along the way. These maps were the only ones used for almost 75 years. In five months the group traveled nearly 1,800 miles and explored much of western Colorado.

"By 1800, Spain had decided to give up trying to get the land in eastern Colorado since it had been claimed by France. Spain claimed only the western and southern parts of what is now Colorado."

The Louisiana Purchase

"The land in eastern Colorado, claimed by France, was called the *Louisiana Territory*. Little was done by the French to try to find out what the area was like. A few French trappers and traders had traveled through eastern Colorado, trading with the Indians. No towns were built by the French in this area. In 1803, France needed some money. *Napoleon Bonaparte* sold this land for nearly 15 million dollars. When the United States bought this land, it almost doubled the size of our country," said Mr. Brown.

"Fifteen million dollars! That is a lot of money," interrupted Maria.

"It sure is, but the Louisiana Territory was a very big area," said Mr. Brown. "The United States really paid only about 3 cents an acre for this land. Now, that is a real bargain.

"*Thomas Jefferson* was president of the United States when this purchase was made," continued Mr. Brown. "President Jefferson wanted to learn as much as he could about this piece of land he had bought. He sent two expeditions into this new territory to explore. Two men named *Lewis and Clark* would lead an exploration of the northern part of the Louisiana Purchase. They were to try to find a water route to the Pacific Ocean."

Zebulon Pike

Pike and his men were not able to climb Pikes Peak because of the deep snow.
(Credit: C.H.S.)

"A second group led by **Zebulon Pike** was to explore the southern part of the Louisiana Purchase. Pike and his men left St. Louis, Missouri, on July 15, 1806. Their main goal was to find the source, or beginning, of the **Red River**. It was believed that this was the boundary between the Louisiana Purchase and Spanish land.

"They crossed Kansas and followed the Arkansas River into Colorado. As they traveled they collected plants, animals, and minerals. Pike also kept a journal telling about the things they saw.

"Pike first spotted the mountain that was to be named after him about two o'clock in the afternoon on November 15th. He said it looked like a small blue cloud. The men were really glad to see mountains. They had been traveling for almost three months across the dry plains. For several days as they traveled toward the mountains, they felt as if they were not getting any closer to them. Finally, they arrived at the base of the peak.

"On November 27th, Pike decided he wanted to climb the peak. He began climbing a nearby mountain in an effort to reach the taller peak. It took two and a half days. The men were not prepared for winter and climbing through the snow was too difficult. Pike decided that the mountain was too tall. He was sure that no one would ever be able to get to the top of what he thought was an 18,000 foot peak.

"They needed to continue to explore the area. The men made winter clothes and shoes out of buffalo skins, beaver skins, and deer hide. They took what food they could and followed the Arkansas River to where **Cañon City** would one day be built. From there, Pike followed the Arkansas River and discovered the **Royal Gorge**. They couldn't get across the gorge because of the very steep walls.

"As the group traveled through **South Park**, a cold wind blew. There was not

This is what Pikes Peak may have looked like to Zebulon Pike.
(Credit: C.H.S.)

70

enough food for the horses, so the men were no longer able to ride. They continued to travel on foot. It was a cold and difficult journey. The men spent Christmas Day trying to keep warm around a pitch-pine fire near what would one day be the town of *Buena Vista.*

"It was too cold for them to follow the Arkansas River any further. Pike knew they would not be able to find the **headwaters** of the Arkansas River like President Jefferson had asked him to do."

"What do you mean by headwaters?" asked Chelsea.

"The headwaters of a river is the source or beginning point of that river," explained Mr. Brown.

"The men struggled on through the deep snow. They turned south trying to find the Red River. They didn't know that the Red River actually begins in Texas and then forms the boundary between Oklahoma and Texas. They were not even close to the headwaters of the Red River.

"Since Pike believed the Red River was the southern boundary of the Louisiana Purchase, he thought they were still in American territory. Pike and his men stopped and set up a temporary fort. It was here that a group of Spanish soldiers found and arrested them."

"Why did they arrest them?" interrupted Keith.

"Pike and his men were in territory claimed by Spain," explained Mr. Brown. "The Spaniards said that Pike and his men were spies.

"Pike's journal was taken from him and he and his men were taken to Santa Fe for questioning. They were then taken to Mexico. It was July of 1807 before Pike was set free. He never returned to Colorado. Pike was sometimes called the 'lost pathfinder' because he really didn't know where he was. There were no maps or guide books of this area."

"Did Pike ever get back his journal?" asked Lindsay.

"No, but he began making notes while he was in prison. Then, when he was released, he rewrote his journal from memory."

ROYAL GORGE, ARKANSAS CAÑON

Steep cliffs rise above the Arkansas River at the Royal Gorge.
(Credit: C.H.S.)

Buena Vista

Stephen H. Long

This picture of Stephen Long was painted by Juan Menchaca.
(Credit: C.H.S.)

North Platte River
Greeley.
Longs Peak ▲ Denver .
South Platte River
. Colorado Springs

Dr. Edwin James sketched this picture of the Rocky Mountains in 1820.
(Credit: C.H.S.)

"In 1820, ***Major Stephen H. Long*** was asked by the army to make a quick trip into the western mountains. He became the first American to explore northern Colorado. He had been sent to find out if this area would be a good place for people to live. His job was also to try to find the source of the ***Platte River***.

"It was a hot summer when Long and 18 men crossed the plains. The group included a map maker, a zoologist, a doctor, a botanist-geologist, a naturalist, and a landscape painter. Since they were mounted on horseback, they made very good time. Everything was dry and brown. Major Long decided that no one would ever be able to farm or live in that area. Long's map maker made a map of the places they visited and saw in Colorado. On his map he wrote ***'Great American Desert'*** across the high plains area of eastern Colorado. Many people believed Long. For years they thought that Colorado would not be a good place to live. They sure were wrong.

"By the end of June, the group could see the Rocky Mountains. They saw a mountain that they thought was Pike's 'great peak', but what they saw actually would later be called ***Longs Peak***.

"The group traveled through the areas that would become ***Greeley*** and ***Denver***. They traveled up and over the divide into the area where ***Colorado Springs*** is today. One member of the party, ***Edwin James***, decided to try to climb Pikes Peak. With two companions he started out. Each man carried a blanket, some buffalo meat, and a pound of corn meal. They spent the night on the side of the mountain and by mid afternoon the next day they had reached the top. They became the first white men on record to climb the famous peak. In honor of this fact, Long wanted to call the mountain, James Peak. In 1843, **John C. Fremont** put the name Pike's Peak on his maps and that became the official name. Today, Pikes Peak is written without the apostrophe.

Edwin James climbed Pikes Peak in 1820.
(Credit: C.H.S.)

"From Pikes Peak they continued south toward the Arkansas River. Part of the group was to follow the Arkansas River and head back to Fort Smith. Long led the other part of the group to try to find the Red River. They finally found a river they thought was the Red River. They followed it only to find that it emptied into the Arkansas River. They had been on the **Canadian River** and not the Red River.

"Long's group did not do what they had set out to do. They did not find the sources of the Platte, the Arkansas, or the Red rivers. They did bring back lots of information about Indian tribes in the area. They also brought back samples of the plants they found growing in the area. The reports Long gave of his trip would affect the area that would become Colorado for many years."

Santa Fe Trail

"In 1822, **William Becknell** heard that Mexico wanted to trade with other countries. He led a group of pack animals loaded with trade goods from St. Louis to New Mexico. He traveled over the very steep **Raton Pass** that is between Colorado and New Mexico."

"I thought they wanted to trade with Mexico. Why did he want to go to New Mexico?" asked Joe.

"At that point in time, New Mexico was not a part of the United States," said Mr. Brown. "It was land claimed by Mexico. Santa Fe was a large town and had become the center of trade between Mexico and the United States.

"On his second trip to Santa Fe, Becknell decided to use three wagons instead of pack animals. He knew it would be difficult to get wagons over the very steep Raton Pass. He

SANTA FE TRAIL

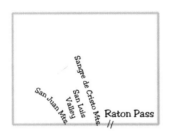

Raton Pass is between
Colorado and New Mexico.
(Credit: C.H.S.)

followed the **Cimarron River** around the mountains. The path he followed would become one of the routes of the **Santa Fe Trail**. It was called the **Cimarron Cut-Off**. The problem with the cut-off was that it went through Comanche Indian Territory. The Comanche would attack any small group that came into their territory. Smaller groups of travelers or ones using pack animals usually chose the Raton Pass because it was safer. People with wagons or larger groups would take the Cimarron Cut-Off.

"William Becknell earned the nickname 'Father of the Santa Fe Trail.' For the next 20 years, the Santa Fe Trail became the main route for people wanting to travel from Missouri to New Mexico."

John Charles Fremont

"In 1848, some businessmen from St. Louis hired John C. Fremont to find a route from St. Louis to the Pacific. They wanted to build a railroad and they wanted Fremont to find the best route. This would be the fourth expedition led by Fremont. **Kit Carson** had been his guide for the first three. Fremont hoped to have Carson be his guide again, but Carson was not available. **'Parson' Bill Williams**, who had been a mountain man, took the job.

"It was winter time and many of the men, who knew what winter in the mountains was like, tried to get Fremont to wait. Fremont wanted to make the trip in winter. He wanted to find out if it was possible for a railroad to run through the Rockies in the winter. After crossing the **Sangre de Cristo Mountains** they went through the **San Luis Valley**. From there they headed up the **San Juan Mountains**. They got to almost 12,000 feet. Here the snowdrifts were very deep and they were not able to go any further.

This painting shows John C. Fremont and Kit Carson who was Fremont's guide for the first three expeditions.
(Credit: C.H.S.)

74

"The group started back. They headed south to get out of the snow. One third of the men died before they reached safety. Fremont lost most of his equipment and all of his mules. Some people blamed the failure of this expedition on Williams. They said he was not a good guide. Others said that Fremont was to blame because he did not listen to his guide. No one really knows for sure."

This drawing by Frederic Remington shows John C. Fremont and his men around a camp fire. *(Credit: C.H.S.)*

Captain John Gunnison

"In 1853, *Captain John Gunnison* was assigned by Congress to explore and map the central Rockies. Gunnison took 62 men and 18 wagons pulled by six mules each. He also had a wagon that carried instruments and an ambulance wagon. The group moved up the Santa Fe Trail and into the San Luis Valley. They then moved up and over *Cochetopa Pass* and down to the *Gunnison River*. From there they traveled on to the 'Grand River' which would become known as the Colorado.

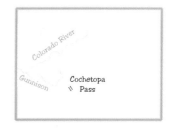

"It was not easy traveling. They had to chop down trees and move large rocks in order to get the wagons through. Gunnison decided that the only way a train could come through the mountains would be with lots of very expensive tunnels.

"Once they reached the Colorado River they traveled west into the Utah desert. It was here that they were attacked by Paiute Indians. Captain Gunnison and seven of his men were killed.

"That is just a few of the people who came into Colorado to learn about this new area. Next time we will begin to look at the role of the mountain men in the history of Colorado. Right now, let's get cleaned up and go outside for recess."

This painting of John Gunnison is by Juan Menchaca. *(Credit: C.H.S.)*

75

What Did You Learn?

1. According to the written records we have, who was the first European to come to Colorado?
2. Which European first discovered the Arkansas River?
3. Which two European countries once claimed to own parts of Colorado?
4. How much did the United States pay for the Louisiana Territory?
5. What are the headwaters of a river?
6. How tall did Zebulon Pike think Pikes Peak was?
7. Why did the Spaniards arrest Zebulon Pike?
8. What was the name of the man from Long's party who first made it to the top of Pikes Peak?
9. What was the main goal of Long's expedition?
10. What name did Long give to the eastern plains?
11. What was the goal of John Fremont's 4th expedition?
12. What area was John Gunnison asked to explore?
13. Why did Becknell use the Cimmarron Cutoff on his second trip over the Santa Fe Trail?

What Do You Think?

1. If you were an early explorer in Colorado what would you have liked to discover? Why?
2. What do you think Pike's men did when they discovered the Great Sand Dunes?
3. Why do you think the men in Long's group were able to climb Pikes Peak when Pike was not able to climb it?

Use Your Imagination

1. Pretend you are the first explorer to come to Colorado. Write in your journal what you think you would have seen and done.
2. Jefferson had a dream to make the United States bigger. What dream do you have for your future? Write about your plans to make your dream come true.
3. Pretend you are Pike. You have just been captured by the Spanish. Your journal has been taken from you. Write a new journal describing your trip.

Chapter 6
Fur Trappers and Traders

Mr. Brown turned on the overhead projector. The following ad flashed up on the screen:

Job Opportunity

Needed: Brave people to go to Mars

Ready to face the unknown

Chance to earn lots of money

Contact: General Henry T. Smith

Pentagon, Washington D.C.

"How many of you would want to answer an ad like this?" asked Mr. Brown. A half dozen hands went up. "Well Paul," said Mr. Brown, "why would you answer that ad?"

"I think it would be a blast to go to Mars," said Paul.

"Adam, I noticed that you didn't put your hand up. How do you feel about it?" Mr. Brown asked.

"You could get killed doing something like that. Who knows what might be up there. There might be Martians," stated Adam. "I'd rather be a pro baseball player."

"As you can see different people want different things," explained Mr. Brown. "That's how it was back in the 1800s too. Some men were willing to take risks because they wanted to explore the West. Others were very happy staying where they were. Would you believe that something as simple as a hat could make someone want to risk their life?"

Types of Beaver Hats

1650
Quaker

1750
Tricorne

1790
High-crown

1800
Bicorne

1820
Top Hat

1850
Stovepipe

Beaver fur was used to make many different styles of felt hats.
(Credit:Kathy Petersen)

Beaver Fever

"Hats made from felt had become very popular in Europe. All the gentlemen wanted to wear one. These hats were expensive because the felt was made from beaver fur. This made beaver skins worth a lot of money. The explorers, Pike and Long, wrote about the many beaver ponds they saw while they were in Colorado. This was very exciting news back in St. Louis. There was an ad for men to go and hunt beaver in the West. It took men who wanted adventure and were not afraid of the unknown to take this job.

"Many men thought that trapping and trading for beaver would be an exciting adventure. Others thought that they could become very rich trapping beaver."

"I think it would have been an exciting life," said Yeong Se.

"Well, let me tell you a little bit about their lives and then you can decide if you think you would like to have been a mountain man."

Life of the Mountain Men

"The men who trapped for beaver skins had to be tough to survive. Mountain men led a very hard life. The average mountain man lived only about three years in the rugged Rocky Mountains. Danger seemed to await them around every corner. Wild animals, Indians, storms, accidents, sickness, and starvation were always there to threaten their lives. Some of the tougher men lived in the mountains for as many as twenty years. Some of the weaker ones didn't even last one year.

"By 1830 there were almost 600 trappers or mountain men living in the Rocky Mountains. Most of these men gave up their civilized ways when they began living in the mountains."

"What do you mean by civilized ways?" asked Erin.

"It means that they didn't live like people in a town or city would live," Mr. Brown explained. "They lived a wild type of life. They changed their type of clothing, food, speech, and habits. First, let me tell you a little about their clothing."

Clothing

"Their clothes were usually made of buckskin with long fringes. They were often covered with porcupine quills and Indian bead work. Along with this they wore moccasins and a felt hat. They usually had a knife and a tomahawk, or ax, tucked into their belt.

"Their buckskin suits would last three or four years. Their clothes were usually never washed or cleaned during that time."

"You mean they didn't wash their clothes for three years!" exclaimed Abigail. "Oh, yuck! That's disgusting."

"Well, I read somewhere that some of the mountain men never even took off their buckskin suits until they put on a new one. Most of these rugged men let their hair and beards grow long," said Mr. Brown. He held up a picture of a mountain man.

"Wow, he looks like a wild man," said Bryan.

"If you think they looked wild, wait until you hear what they ate!" Mr. Brown added.

A mountain man and his ponies.
(Credit: C.H.S.)

Food

"It seemed to be either feast or famine for the mountain men. Sometimes they had more than they needed to eat. At other times they were near starvation. They ate elk, deer, bear, antelope, panther, and other animals. Sometimes they ate dog, horse, beaver, ants, crickets, and snakes."

"Oh, Mr. Brown. You're teasing us," said Maria. "They didn't really eat ants, crickets, and snakes, did they?"

"Yes they did," he said. "They had to eat what they could find. When they were really hungry, some mountain men even ate their own moccasins. Buffalo meat seemed to be the favorite food. Sometimes they ate all parts of it, including the intestines and the brain." The whole class groaned.

"They sometimes even drank the blood," Mr. Brown continued. "The tongue was thought to be the best part by many. Since buffalo were not mountain animals, the mountain men usually had to settle for other types of meat. They didn't eat bread or vegetables very often. In times of plenty they would eat seven to eight pounds of meat a day. Some could eat as much as ten pounds of meat at one meal. That would be like eating forty quarter pound hamburgers without the buns."

"That would be a pretty big meal!" exclaimed Erin. "I can't even finish one hamburger."

"I TOOK YE FOR AN INJIN."

Drawing of two mountain men by Frederic Remington. (Credit: Idaho Historical Society)

Shelter and Family Life

"Where did the mountain men live, Mr. Brown?" asked Tim.

"Their home was often a lean-to shelter. It was covered with branches and was open in the front. A campfire was built in the opening. Meat and traps were hung from racks made from the antlers of deer or elk. In winter, a group of trappers might build a rough log cabin or an Indian type tipi to live in."

"Did their families live there too?" asked Kelli.

"Most of the men who came to trap in the West were not married when they came," answered Mr. Brown. "Some of the mountain men chose Indian women as wives. The women cooked the food, skinned the animals, and made clothes. Often they cut the wood, too. They worked really hard."

"Why would they marry a mountain man if they had to work so hard?" asked Michael.

"Actually, these women usually had an easier life than the wives of the Indians in their own tribes. They received nicer clothes, steel tools, and often a good horse of their own.

"Many of the mountain men who left the West would divorce their Indian wives. They did this in the Indian fashion. They would just tell their wife to go home. The Indian woman would then return to her own tribe with all of her belongings. She would have a special high status in her tribe and would usually marry again very soon. Some of the mountain men who stayed in the West remarried their Indian wives in a church."

Trapping

"We don't want to forget the reason the mountain men lived up in the mountains like this," he continued.

"They wanted to trap beaver," said Juan.

"That's right," said Mr. Brown. "There were two main seasons when the mountain men could hunt and trap beaver. The first was from the beginning of spring through early summer. Beaver fur was too thin in late summer to be worth much. The second season was from September until the streams and ponds froze over. It was impossible to trap in the ice and snow of winter.

Beaver fur was thicker in fall and spring.
(Credit: C.H.S.)

"Some mountain men worked alone. It was really dangerous to work alone. If they had an accident such as a broken leg, they probably would not live. There would be no one to go get help for them. This is why many of them worked in pairs or in small groups."

"How did they catch the beaver?" asked Jessie.

"The mountain men would take a trap and set it with the strong powerful jaws open. A five foot chain would be fastened to a nearby tree, or fastened with a stick under water. **Castor**, or **castoreum**, a liquid that comes from the beaver, was used for bait. When the beaver touched the trap, it would snap shut on its paw. He would try to swim to escape the danger. The trap would go in the water with the beaver and the weight of the trap would cause him to drown.

Mountain men usually carried between 6-8 traps.
(Courtesy: Matt March)

"A trapper would usually return later in the day to check the traps. He would take the dead beaver out and reset the trap. Then he would skin the beaver. He usually took only the skin, the castoreum gland, the tail, and the brains back to camp."

"Why did they take the tail and the brains?" asked Joe.

"The tail was very good to eat," responded Mr. Brown. "The brains were used to help prepare the skins."

Beaver pelts were often stretched on a willow frame to dry.

"Back at camp the trapper or his wife would stretch the skin over a willow frame. The skin would be scraped clean of all the meat and fat and then dried. Sometimes they were stretched over a smoldering fire to help them dry out. The skin would be softened by rubbing it with the brains of the animal.

"A beaver pelt was called a '**plew.**' This name came from the French word 'plus' which means pelt. A pelt, or a plew, weighed about a pound and a half. They were sold for about $4.00 a pound. A trapper could make from $1,000 to $2,000 in a season, which was good money.

"When the trapper had eighty to one hundred skins, he would fold the furs into a pack. The pack of plews had to be **cached**," said Mr. Brown.

"You mean like you cash a check?" said Kate.

"It sounds like it," said Mr. Brown, as he wrote the word on the board. "It is pronounced cashed, but it is not spelled the same way."

"What does it mean?" asked Kate.

"It is a French word meaning hiding place," said Mr. Brown. "The trappers were very careful to make a well-hidden cache. Often they would dig a deep hole near a stream. The hole would be wider at the bottom than at

Setting traps could be cold, hard work.
(Credit: C.H.S.)

the top. The skins or plews would be placed in the bottom of the hole. They were covered with a buffalo robe and then with sod and dirt. Branches and another layer of soil came next. This was topped by the original soil. The trappers tried to make it look like no one had dug there.

"All this did not always protect the furs. Indians or other men often found them in spite of all the care taken to hide them carefully. Many furs were also ruined by water leaking into the cache."

Rendezvous

"When all the beaver in one section of a stream had been trapped, the mountain men would move their camp to a fresh area and begin again. Once the trapping season was over, the mountain men gathered their furs together. Many would head to a **rendezvous**."

"What's a 'ron-de-voo'?" asked Zach.

"In 1822 a man named ***William Ashley*** formed the Rocky Mountain Fur Company. He hired men to work for him. Before they went out to work in the spring, a place was chosen where they would meet in July. Lots of supplies were brought to this place. The mountain men and Indians would bring their furs to trade for supplies. Since many of the traders were French, the meeting became known as a rendezvous. This is the French word that means, 'place of meeting.' The rendezvous was usually held in a flat mountain valley such as Green River in Wyoming."

"What did they do at a rendezvous?" asked David.

"The mountain men would trade their furs for money and supplies. They needed to get things like powder for their guns, lead for bullets, knives, traps, blankets, salt, and other necessities. The traders charged the trappers very high prices for the supplies. If the trappers had enough furs, they would

The Summer
Rendezvous
*(Credit: Idaho
Historical Society)*

THE SUMMER RENDEZVOUS.

83

The rendezvous was a time for the mountain men to gather and trade.
(Credit: C.H.S.)

also trade for things like watered-down whiskey, trinkets, and other luxuries such as sugar and chocolate.

"The rendezvous was also a big social event for these mountain men. They played games, danced, and had contests of skill. Some of the games and contests they had were very dangerous. Many of the men were hurt while playing these games. Alcohol was popular and the traders sold it at a very high price. Unfortunately many men drank too much. This caused problems at the rendezvous. The mountain men played cards and gambled recklessly at all sorts of games. Some men lost everything. They would gamble away their traps, guns, knives, supplies, and even their wives. Many mountain men would leave the rendezvous with little to show for a year of hard work. A lot of them were even in debt to the fur traders.

"The rendezvous system lasted for about 15 years," Mr. Brown continued. " Many of these traders began to set up trading posts. As more and more trading posts were built, the rendezvous began to die out.

"At the trading posts, supplies were traded for furs and buffalo skins. You could often find a blacksmith, a carpenter, a wheelwright, gunsmith, and hunters at a trading post. They came from all over so many different languages were spoken at these forts. Let me tell you about a few of the trading posts and forts that were set up in Colorado."

Bent's Fort

"***William and Charles Bent*** were brothers who had gone to ***Santa Fe*** to trade. Together with a man named ***Ceran St. Vrain*** they opened a store. After a while they decided to open a trading post on the plains. Here they could trade with the Indians who lived in that area."

"I thought they wanted to trade with the mountain men," said Brink.

"It was the Indians who actually trapped almost 80% of all the furs traded in the West," stated Mr. Brown. "Most of the traders did a lot of business with the Indians.

"The Bent brothers and St. Vrain began to build **Bent's Fort.** It was one of the earliest trading posts in Colorado. Built in 1833, it was located along the **Arkansas River** near the present day town of **La Junta.**

"The fort was built out of large **<u>adobe</u>** bricks. It was 180 feet by 135 feet. The walls were 15 feet high and 4 feet thick at the base. In the southeast and northwest corners, there were round watch towers that were taller than the walls. In the towers there were cannons and small holes for firing rifles. A huge gateway had two heavy plank doors that were covered with sheet iron. Inside, there were rooms, a warehouse, and a corral. When it was completed, Bent's Fort was the largest trading post in the southwest.

"The traders from Bent's Fort would visit Indian camps in the winter. They would trade knives, blankets, iron pots, and other supplies for buffalo robes that the Indians had made as well as other things like beaver pelts and other animal hides. When spring arrived, the buffalo robes and beaver pelts were loaded into wagons and taken back to Missouri. The robes and pelts were sold and the money was used to buy new supplies to bring back for trade.

"Bent's Fort was called the '*Crossroads of the Southwest.*' American Indians, traders, trappers, travelers, and military men all used the fort to buy supplies and to visit with one another. It was a good stopping point along the **Santa Fe Trail.**"

"Is Bent's Fort still there?" wondered Chelsea.

"Actually, they think Mr. Bent blew the fort up," answered Mr. Brown.

"Why would he blow up his own fort?" asked Gania.

William Bent (above)
Charles Bent (below)
(Credit: C.H.S.)

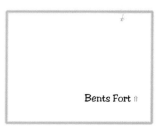

Bents Fort

Bent's Fort
(Credit: C.H.S.)

85

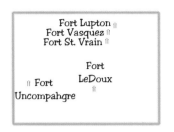

Antoine Robidoux built
Fort Uncompahgre.
(Credit: C.H.S.)

"At one point in time, Bent's Fort became a base for the army. The fort was filled with supplies and soldiers. There were some problems between the settlers, soldiers, and the Indians. During this time, trading stopped. Ceran St. Vrain sold his part of the fort to William Bent, and moved to New Mexico. When the soldiers left his fort, Bent tried to run the fort by himself.

"In 1849 many of the Plains Indians became sick with cholera. They were not able to continue trading at the fort. William Bent became discouraged. The government decided that they wanted to buy the fort from Bent. Bent wanted to sell the fort, but he thought that the price they were offering to pay was way too low. He also knew the government did not have a good record for paying their bills. So instead of selling the fort to the government, some stories say he blew it up.

"He moved down the river, built a new fort and named it ***Fort Wise***. He continued to trade there for a while, then moved to his farm on the ***Purgatoire River***. He died there in 1869. They have rebuilt Bent's Fort, and you can still visit it today."

Fort Uncompahgre

"***Fort Uncompahgre*** was built on the ***Gunnison River*** close to where the city of ***Delta*** is now located. Since this fort was built by ***Antoine Robidoux***, it is sometimes called ***Fort Robidoux***. Mr. Robidoux began trapping in the Green River area around 1825. Robidoux became a Mexican citizen in 1823, so he was allowed to build his fort in Mexican territory. Since this fort was built on the western slope, he did not have much competition. By 1833, he had hired many men to trap for him in the valleys. He became a well-known trader in that area. He traded mainly with the Ute Indians. The Utes had high quality tanned beaver skins."

Fort Le Doux

"This fort was built in the 1830s by a man named ***Le Doux***. It was built out of pine logs placed in the shape of an octagon. It was 144 feet across and had a square courtyard in the middle. Adobe rooms were built inside.

"***Fort Le Doux*** burned to the ground. Le Doux claims that Indians burned it while he was away. Others say his wife was mad because he was away so much, so she left and burned the fort after her."

Fort Lupton

"*Fort Lupton* was built in 1836 by a man named *Lancaster P. Lupton*. Lupton was leading a group of soldiers when he saw Bent's Fort. He noticed that there were not any forts on the Platte River even though this was a busy area for trapping. Lupton went back east and gave up his post in the army. He returned west with a wagon load of trade goods. He built a fort on the banks of the South Platte. He used the same type of adobe bricks that the Bents had used in their fort. He traded with the Indians for nine years. When things began to slow down in the trade business, he began to plant crops and raise livestock."

Fort Lupton (above) was built by Lancaster Lupton (below).
(Credit: C.H.S.)

Fort St. Vrain was built in 1832.
(Credit: C.H.S.)

Painting of Ceran St. Vrain by Waldo Love.
(Credit: C.H.S.)

Fort St. Vrain

"After Fort Lupton was built, the men who built Bent's Fort, decided to build a fort in that same area. It was first called *Fort Lookout*. The name was later changed to *Fort George*, and finally to *Fort St. Vrain*."

Fort Vasquez

Inside Fort Vasquez
(above)
Louis Vasquez (below)
(Credit: C.H.S.)

"*Fort Vasquez* was another fort that was built in Colorado. It was built in 1835 on the **South Platte River** near the present town of **Platteville**. Two well-known mountain men named **Andrew Sublette** and **Louis Vasquez** built the fort. They did a very good business at their trading post. Around the year 1840, they sold their fort to some other people. Within a year, the fort had failed and the new owners had to close it down."

Fort Davy Crockett

"*Fort Davy Crockett* was located in the northwestern part of the state. This fort was a base for beaver trappers. This was not a very nice fort and did not last for very long. The mountain men nicknamed it '*Fort Misery*.'

"That should give you an idea about some of the forts that were in Colorado. Let's go on and learn a little more about some of the men who traded at these posts.

"A few of these trappers became famous. They helped to explore the land we now call Colorado. I would like to tell you a little bit about two of these men," said Mr. Brown.

Fort Davy Crockett
Fort Vasquez
•Platteville

Jim Beckwourth

"*Jim Beckwourth* was born in Virginia in 1798. His mother was a slave. When he turned 25, Mr. Beckwourth headed west to become a mountain man. He made friends with the Indians where he lived. He even helped them fight their enemies. The Indians helped him get beaver and buffalo skins. He lived with the Crow Indians for many years before he moved to Denver. He also was a scout for the army. A newspaper reporter wrote a story about him and he became famous throughout the land.

"When Mr. Beckwourth was 68 years old, the government asked him to talk to the Crow Indians. The government wanted the Indians to stop fighting. Since Mr. Beckwourth had lived with the Indians and was their friend, they thought he might be able to get the Crows to stop fighting. Jim did not return from his visit with the Indians. No one really knows what happened to him."

James Beckwourth made friends
with the Crow Indians.
(Credit: C.H.S.)

Kit Carson

"***Kit Carson*** was born in Kentucky in 1809. He grew up in Missouri. At age 14 he became an apprentice to a saddle maker. An apprentice is someone who learns from someone else how to do a trade. Kit did not like making saddles and ran away when he was 16. The man he was working for offered a reward of one cent for anyone to return Kit to him. Kit joined ***Charles Bent*** who was going to Santa Fe to trade there. Kit met many mountain men and decided that he would like to trap beaver also. He was 5'4" tall and weighed 125 pounds. Even though he was a small man, he was one of the best fur trappers.

Kit Carson, famous mountain man and guide, became a colonel in the army. *(Credit: C.H.S.)*

"There is an interesting story about Kit. It is said that he had just fired at an elk, when he was charged by two grizzly bears. He was able to climb a tree, but dropped his gun. He had to stay in the tree for several hours until the bears gave up trying to shake him out of the tree.

"After the fur trade began to decline, he worked at Bent's Fort as a hunter. He went on Fremont's expedition along the Oregon Trail. He also was a scout for the army. He fought in several battles with the Indians. He served in the army during the Civil War. He lived in New Mexico most of his life, but retired in Colorado. He died at the age of 58 in 1868.

"There were a lot of mountain men who lived and trapped in Colorado," concluded Mr. Brown. "We have talked about just two of them. I think that is enough for now. If any of you are interested, you could find out about some of the other fur traders or trappers. The library has a lot of books to read about the mountain men."

"What ever happened to the mountain men?" asked Ed.

"Good question. It seems that the beaver hat suddenly was no longer popular. The gentlemen in Europe now wanted tall silk hats. The beaver were almost gone because of the heavy trapping. By 1840, most of the mountain men were looking for new adventures. Some of them traded for buffalo skins for a few years. Many of them became guides for the wagon trains that were soon to make their way over the Oregon Trail. Others became scouts for the army.

"You have all been great listeners," said Mr. Brown. "I hope you have learned a lot about what it might have been like to be a fur trapper or trader in early Colorado."

What Did You Learn?

1. Why was beaver fur popular?
2. Tell three things you thought were interesting about the life of a mountain man.
3. Why did many of the mountain men work in small groups instead of alone?
4. Why didn't the mountain men trap beaver all year long?
5. Describe a cache.
6. Tell three things you learned about a rendezvous.
7. Which fort was one of the first in Colorado and was also a good stopping point along the Santa Fe Trail?
8. Which fort was built by Antoine Robidoux?
9. What was a rendezvous?
10. Why were beaver skins suddenly no longer as valuable?

What Do You Think?

1. Would you have liked to have been a mountain man? Why or why not?
2. How do you think Colorado would be different if beaver hats had never been popular?
3. What do you think happened to Jim Beckwourth?
4. What kind of people do you think became fur trappers?
5. How would you hide your pelts if you were a mountain man?

Use Your Imagination

1. Imagine you are a mountain man. Describe one day of your life.
2. Tell what you think it might have been like at a rendezvous.
3. Many mountain men were great story tellers. Write a story you think they might have told.
4. If you were a mountain man what would you want to do when you could no longer trap beaver?

Chapter 7
Spanish Americans

It was a rainy Wednesday afternoon. The class had not been able to go out for recess. Mr. Brown let them play Heads Up-Seven Up until the bell rang. He asked the students to return to their seats so they could begin class.

"But it's my turn to be up," said Yeong Se.

"You can be up first next time," promised Mr. Brown. "Right now, I want all of you to use your imaginations. I want you to imagine that you are at home this evening. Your family is sitting down to dinner. Your father tells you that he has made a big decision. He has been offered a job working on a special space station in outer space. You and your whole family will be leaving for the space station in a few weeks. The problem is that you would have to leave all of your friends. How do you think you would feel?"

"Scared, excited, and a little sad," answered Jessie.

"It is hard to leave your home and friends to go someplace where you don't know what life may be like. Many of the Spanish Americans who lived in New Mexico Territory didn't have enough room for everyone to farm. Many decided to move north to an area now called the **San Luis Valley**. They knew that it could be dangerous. Other Spanish Americans had tried to move there before. They had been driven out by the Utes who were trying to protect their hunting grounds. Now the United States promised it would build a fort in the valley. The army would be able to protect the settlers from the Indians. The Spanish Americans knew it could still be very dangerous. I am sure that it was difficult for the Spanish Americans who lived in New Mexico Territory to leave their homes.

"I found a book the other day. It was written as if it were the journal of a young girl about your age. Her name was Louisa and she lived with her family in a little farming village near Santa Fe in New Mexico Territory. I would like to read a few entries. This may give you an idea of what it was like to move to a new area back in the 1850s. It may also give you a glimpse of what life was like for some of the Spanish Americans who first settled in the San Luis Valley."

Mr. Brown began to read:

July 14, 1851

Today is a really exciting day. Papa says we are moving. We will be going north to find a better place for our family to live and farm. It is too crowded here. We don't have enough room to farm. Our whole family will be going. Mis abuelos (my grandparents) mis tias y tios (my aunts and uncles) mis primos (my cousins) and even mi perro (my dog) will be going. Of course mi Papa y mi Mama (my father and my mother) and mi hermana, Juanita y mi hermano, Pedro (my sister, Juanita and my brother, Pedro) will be going too.

July 17, 1851

Today Papa brought home a new cart. It has two big wheels. The wheels are taller than Juanita. All of the things we will need in our new home like dishes, clothes, pots and pans, Mama's spinning wheel, and Papa's tools will all have to fit into the cart. Each of my uncles and my grandparents will have a cart also. There will be

about 20 carts all together. Papa said that we will have to walk most of the time. It would be too hard for the oxen to have to pull the heavy cart and all of us too.

We are going to *Señor Charles Beaubien's* land called the *Sangre de Cristo Land Grant*. Papa says that the Mexican government gave Señor Beaubien a big area of land if he would get families to come and build a settlement. Señor Beaubien has promised to give some of his land to families who come to his land grant to live and farm.

July 20, 1851

Everything is just about loaded. In our carts we have seeds to plant at our new farm and corn to grind into cornmeal. We also have beans, peppers and some wheat.

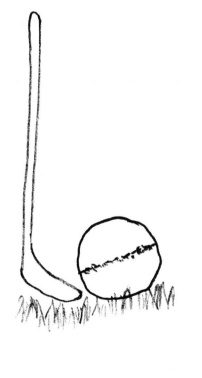

Juanita and I each get to take one doll. Pedro is taking his ball that Mama made for him and his chueco (curved stick) that he uses to hit his ball. Mama made Pedro's ball with the skin from a deer Papa had killed. She sewed two round pieces of skin together and stuffed them with wool from Pedro's sheep. Mama got the wool wet so she could fit more into the ball. When the wool dried, it got bigger and made the ball quite hard.

July 27, 1851

We started north early this morning. Mama drove the team of oxen that pulled the two wheeled cart. Our sheep, two cows, a horse and two pigs, along with all the other families' animals, followed the carts. Papa and some other men walked behind the wagons. The men had a big job trying to keep the animals moving and together. The animals kept stopping to eat and some of them wandered away from the rest. My grandfather rode his burro. Another man rode his horse. The men worked hard to keep the animals together.

I was really tired when Papa said it was time to stop. Everyone put their carts in a circle. That way we have sort of a pen, or corral, to keep the animals safe at night.

July 28, 1851

Papa woke us up really early this morning. Juanita and I helped Mama fix breakfast. We also fixed some things we could eat for lunch since we don't stop to make a fire at noon. Pedro helped to roll up the beds. Our beds are mattresses made of wool. Pedro also helped my grandmother get her cart loaded. By the time we had everything on the carts the men had the animals ready to move.

The animals really slow us down. We only came about seven miles today. Papa says it will take us about a month to get to our new home.

August 2, 1851

Today we went about 9 miles. Mama cooked mush made from the corn I ground . It really tasted good. Papa says we have to be very careful. We are getting near the area where the Indians hunt and we can only have a fire for a short time each night. Tonight is Papa's turn to stay awake and watch. About midnight my uncle Federico will come to stand guard so Papa can sleep.

August 19, 1851

Papa is really upset with the pigs. They keep lying down to rest. I think we may eat pig for dinner tomorrow if they don't move better. Papa and the pigs were almost three miles

behind the first wagon when we stopped tonight.

We are almost to our new land and Papa wants to get there so we can get our house built before it snows. I will be glad to sleep in a house again instead of under our cart.

August 23, 1851

We finally made it to the valley where we will live. What a beautiful place. There is lots of sagebrush, rabbitbrush, greasewood, yucca and prickly pear cactus. The foothills are covered with juniper and pinion trees. Further up the mountains are aspen, fir and spruce trees. Papa says this will be a wonderful place to farm.

August 25, 1851

Today we arrived at the place where we will build our home. Papa says we made really good time. We were all so glad, we knelt down to pray. We gave thanks that we had a safe trip.

Today is the festival of San Luigi. Everyone decided that we would name our settlement *San Luis* in honor of this saint.

Tomorrow Papa will begin to build a jacale (log house) for us to live in.

August 26, 1851

We unloaded the carts so the men can haul the poles we will need to build our jacales. Papa will stand the poles up side by side. Juanita, Pedro and I will help fill in the cracks between the poles with mud. The roof will be flat. Papa will lay more poles across the top. We will then put leaves and dirt on top of the poles. Mama will hang some of her woven cloth across under the roof. This will keep the leaves and dirt from falling through the poles. We will live in the jacale only until Papa can build us a home of adobe like our house in Santa Fe.

September 7, 1851

Our jacale is finished. The jacale keeps out most of the wind and rain so it is better than sleeping under the cart. It is not as warm as an adobe house. Our old adobe home was warm in winter and cool in the summer.

Papa will begin to make the bricks for our adobe house soon. Juanita, Pedro and I will help to drive the oxen back and forth through a shallow pit to mix the adobe. Clay is mixed with straw, sand and water. We can only do this on warm days. When the clay is mixed we will put it into wet forms made of wood. Papa will stack the bricks on end to dry. It takes several weeks for them to dry.

December 15, 1851

Papa says that when we get our adobe house finished we will begin to build a church. On cold days he has been carving a bulto (figure of a saint) to give to our new church. This year we will just have a small fiesta (celebration) for Christmas because our church is not built.

December 31, 1851

Today is the last day of the old year. In Santa Fe we would have had a special mass and fiesta tonight. Next year, when we have our new church, we will have mass again.

Mama made me a new skirt of jerga (heavy woolen cloth). She is making me a blouse of sabanilla (finer woolen cloth). My summer clothes are made of sabanilla. Papa has a new suit made from deerskin. His old pants were made from jerga. Mama has a beautiful rebozo (silk scarf) which she wears over her head and I have a tapalo (shawl) which I can wear over my head. Mama is also making new moccasins for us from some of the tanned deer hides.

January 15, 1852

We have had very little snow this winter. Papa says that is good since he has been able to make lots of adobe bricks. Next winter we will be in our adobe house. That will be much warmer. Papa says the walls will be about 30 inches thick. The adobe bricks take much longer to dry in the winter than they do in the summer.

February 3, 1852

Papa says we have enough bricks to begin our house. The men have put a stone foundation down. We can see what the plaza will look like. All of the families will build their houses to form the plaza. That is a square with a large

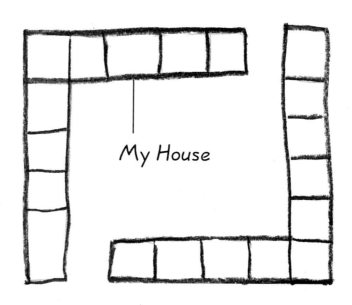

My House

open area, or patio, in the middle. There will be two openings in the square plaza. These openings can be closed at night or in case of an Indian attack, by putting a heavy wooden gate across them. Our home will be on the north side of the plaza and will have three rooms. My grandparents will have only two rooms on the east side. They will be next to my Uncle Federico. Uncle Juan will be next to us on the north side of the plaza. It will be great having a large patio where all my cousins and friends can play games.

The men will also build a horno (beehive shaped oven for cooking) in the patio.

February 23, 1852

The plaza will be built near the river. The men plan to dig a well in the middle of the patio. It will be nice not to have to go to the river for our water. Each of my uncles will have land to farm. We will keep all of our animals together in a pasture beyond the farms. Once the plaza is finished we can bring the animals into the patio at night, if we need to, in order to keep them safe.

March 9, 1852

Our adobe home is coming along nicely. Papa says he must stop work on the house until the fields are planted. He will plant peas, beans, potatoes, chilies, corn, and wheat. He has planted some fruit trees. It will be a few years before we get any fruit.

Papa's plow is made of wood. The oxen help to pull the plow through the soil. It is hard work. Papa says a metal plow would be better, but metal costs too much. If we can get enough water to our field we should have good crops.

Our farm is about 200 vargas wide(a varga is about 2½ feet) and several hundred vargas long. It runs from the river up almost to the foot of the mountains. The land in the mountains is for all of us to use. We can take our animals up there to graze in the mountain pastures and we can cut different kinds of wood that we need.

April 1, 1852

Yesterday, the men sheared our sheep. Mama and the other women have been very busy washing all the wool. Juanita and I have helped to spread the clean wool out to dry. Mama will stuff a new mattress for Pedro with some of the wool. She will also spin some into yarn.

Mama can't weave any more cloth until Papa builds a new loom for us. The old loom was too big to bring with us. Mama will have to wait until he is not so busy in the fields and working on our home. Once Papa gets our new loom made, Mama will weave the yarn into cloth. We have found some special plants that will help us make the yarn different colors. Rabbitbrush makes a pretty yellow.

March 27, 1852

The weather is warmer now. Soon all the animals will be taken up into the mountain pasture for the summer. Some of the older boys will take them and stay to take care of them until early September when they will be brought down again.

April 1, 1852

The men have been digging a large ditch to carry water to all the farms. This way everyone can get water to their plants. Papa says this is called irrigation.

April 10, 1852

The men finished digging the big ditch. It will be called The *San Luis People's Ditch*. Everyone will dig acequias (little ditches) to carry the water to their fields. Each family has to keep their acequias clean and Papa says that no one is supposed to build an acequia above his. The people who came first have the first right to the water.

July 13, 1852

We are finishing up our home. Papa built a tarima (bench) along one wall. The tarima is made of adobe. During the daytime we can roll up our wool mattresses and put them on the tarima. He is also building adobe shelves on the wall. These will hold our dishes. We have all been busy putting zoquete (mud) over all the walls.

August 10, 1852

We finally moved into our new adobe home. I helped Mama grind some of our corn into cornmeal. We took turns using our mano and metate to grind the corn. It is very hard work. We will make atole (thick mush) from the blue cornmeal. Mama will also make tortillas.

Mama cooks in her big kettles over the fire in the fireplace. We have several sheepskins that we can sit on. At mealtime we all put our sheepskins around the fireplace.

August 12, 1852

Papa and Pedro worked out in the field all day long again today.

Mama, Juanita and I have so many things to do in the house each day there is little time to play. Grinding corn is hard and it takes a lot of time. This must be done before we can do the cooking. We also have to make our own soap. Tomorrow all of the women will be making candles.

August 24, 1852

One of the men is talking about building a grist mill. It will be right beside the river. There will be a waterwheel to help turn the big stones. The stones will grind our wheat into flour. It will really make baking easier when we don't have to grind the flour with our mano and metate. Everyone in San Luis will use the grist mill.

It will soon be time to harvest all of our crops. Papa says we have had a good year. Right after harvest we will begin making adobe bricks for our church.

December 4, 1852

Today was a really nice day. My cousins and I played games in the patio. One nice thing about the winter is there is not as much work to do. It was fun to see Grandpa sitting in the sun. After our game, we asked him for a story. It was a really special time.

January 6, 1853

Today Papa finished building Mama's new loom. Mama was really happy. We have a lot of yarn ready to weave. Mama is going to teach me how to use the loom.

February 17, 1853

Today a priest from Santa Fe came. We had our first mass in our new church. Soon we hope to have our own priest here in San Luis.

March 9, 1853

Since our church is finished, the men will begin building a school. I hope I am not too old to be able to go. Usually only the younger children go. I love school so much maybe Papa will let me go in the winter when there is not so much work.

Mr. Brown put the book down. " I hope that gives you some idea of what it might have been like to live in the San Luis Valley in the 1850s," he said. "San Luis was the first town settled in Colorado.

"In 1852 the army built **Fort Massachusetts**. It was later moved and called **Fort Garland**. Fort Garland played a very important part in the lives of the settlers. **Kit Carson** was the commander of Fort Garland for several years.

"In 1857 **Dario Gallegos** started the first store in San Luis. He only had a few things like material, brown sugar, coffee, chocolate, and some different kinds of grains. This made it so the people of San Luis did not have to make or grow everything they needed.

"In 1863 Señor Charles Beaubien agreed to sell his claim to the Sangre de Cristo Grant to **William Gilpin**. Gilpin, the first territorial governor, had just left office. As part of his agreement to sell, Beaubien insisted that the rights of the settlers would always be honored. But Gilpin and the Colorado courts chose to make their own rules. There have been many lawsuits over this land. The common land in the mountains, that was supposed to be for the use of all the settlers, was sold. The people who bought the mountain land tried to keep the settlers from using it. This made it really hard for the farmers. They needed the mountain land to pasture their animals, to hunt wildlife, and to cut wood.

"The farmers have also lost many of their water rights. This makes it harder and harder for them to farm and make a living on the land that has been in their family for almost 150 years.

"**La Gente**, as the Spanish Americans often call themselves, are proud of the part they have played in the development of Colorado. Some of their influence on Colorado can be seen in the number of places which still have Spanish names. Can you think of any names that probably came from the Spanish," asked Mr. Brown.

"How about **Pueblo**?" asked Kevin.

"Good," said Mr. Brown. "Pueblo is Spanish for town or village. Are there any others?"

Pueblo •

Fort Garland • Fort Massachusetts
• San Luis

"The San Luis Valley, the **San Juan Mountains**, and the **Sangre de Cristo Mountains**," said Abigail.

"I think **La Junta** is Spanish," said Kelsey.

"That's right. It means the junction," answered Mr. Brown.

"Is **Cimarron** a Spanish name?" asked Paul.

"Yes," answered Mr. Brown. "It means unruly or wild. **Fruita** is another Spanish word. It means fruit. As you travel around Colorado you will run into lots of Spanish names. You will also see some French names. For example, **Laporte** is French for the door and **Cache La Poudre** means where the powder is hidden. Sometimes you will see Indian names such as **Saguache, Uncompahgre**, and **Ouray**. All of these groups of people and many more played an important role in the exploration and development of Colorado."

Spanish Americans often hung peppers to dry outside their adobe homes.
(Credit: C.H.S.)

These children are standing next to a horno that was used for baking.
(Credit: C.H.S.)

107

What Did You Learn?

1. What happened to the first groups of Spanish Americans who tried to settle in the San Luis Valley?

2. What was the name of the first town to be settled in Colorado?

3. Why did the Spanish Americans want to leave Santa Fe and move north?

4. Who owned the Sangre de Cristo Land Grant?

5. About how long did the trip from Santa Fe to the San Luis Valley take?

6. What was the name of the first type of housing they built in the San Luis Valley?

7. What is adobe made from?

8. About how long does it take the big adobe bricks to dry?

9. Why will the adobe house be a good place to live?

10. Why was the common land important to the settlers?

What Do You Think?

1. Why do you think only the younger children went to school? Tell how you would feel about a rule like this. Why?

2. What do you think it would be like to live in a plaza with all of your family, aunts, uncles, cousins, and grandparents? What would be good and what would be hard about living so close to all of your family?

3. The early Spanish American children had lots of jobs to do to help the family. Do you think they had to work harder than you? Why or why not?

Use Your Imagination

1. If you were moving and could take only one thing besides your clothes, what would you take? Why? What would you do with the things you could not take?

2. Pretend you are moving from Santa Fe to the San Luis Valley in 1851. Describe one day of your journey.

3. Pretend you are a Ute Indian in 1851. Settlers are building homes and starting farms on your hunting grounds. Tell how you feel and what you think would be the best thing to do.

Chapter 8
Gold

"We have a problem," said Mr. Brown one morning. "The boys and girls in our school left popcorn bags all over our playground yesterday. We are going to lose popcorn day if this happens again. I thought maybe we could take fifteen minutes and get it all cleaned up. I have three trash bags. We'll divide into three teams and the team that picks up the most trash will win a prize."

Mr. Brown divided the class, and the children hurried out to the playground. They worked quickly. When they came back in, they found that Joe's team had won.

"Here is your prize," said Mr. Brown. He handed Joe five pennies.

"You've got to be kidding, Mr. Brown!" exclaimed Joe. "We worked hard. Five cents isn't very much. What good is five cents? There are seven of us on my team."

"You're right, five cents isn't something that many people would work very hard for. But I know about some men who would work all day and maybe only earn a few cents," said Mr. Brown.

"Why would they work so hard for only a few pennies?" asked Abigail.

"They had big dreams of striking it rich and becoming wealthy," continued Mr. Brown. "They always hoped that they would find more the next day. Let me tell you their story.

"In 1849, gold was discovered in California. Thousands of **prospectors** rushed to California to strike it rich."

"What are prospectors, Mr. Brown?" asked Zach.

"Prospectors are people who are looking or searching for something. In this case, the men were looking for gold," answered Mr. Brown. "These men were called '*Forty-Niners*,' because they all traveled to California in the year 1849. Some prospectors struck it rich, but most were not so lucky. Many began to look for gold in other places. Some of the prospectors had passed through the area that would become Colorado on their way to California. They had stopped long enough to pan for gold in a few of the

rivers. They did discover small amounts of gold, but not enough to keep them from going on to California. As the gold began to run out in California, some of the men remembered the gold they had seen in Colorado. They decided to head back there."

Pikes Peak Gold Rush

William Green Russell found gold at the mouth of Dry Creek.
(Credit: C.H.S.)

"**William Green Russell** and his two brothers **Levi** and **Oliver** had been to California to search for gold. They returned to Georgia and decided to organize a group of men to explore the Rocky Mountain area. In February of 1858, the three brothers and six other men began their journey. As they moved along the **Santa Fe Trail**, others began to join them. Pretty soon there were 104 people on their way to Colorado. When they reached **Bent's Fort** they began to travel northwest to where **Cherry Creek** flows into the **South Platte River**.

"They did not have much success panning for gold on Cherry Creek, **Ralston Creek,** or other streams that flowed from the mountains. After 20 days most of the men had left. William, his brothers, and ten others stayed. In July of 1858, they found gold at the mouth of **Dry Creek**. They were able to pan several hundred dollars' worth of gold out of Dry Creek.

"Around this same time, a group of men from Lawrence, Kansas, heard about gold around Pikes Peak. Once they arrived, they began to look for gold. They did not have any luck, so they decided that they would start a town."

"Why did they want to build a town?" asked Erin.

"They knew that if there was a gold rush to this area, they could make a lot of money by developing a town. The miners would need food, supplies, and places to stay. If they built a town, they could provide these things for the miners.

SANTA FE TRAIL

"They picked a place north of Dry Creek and named it **Montana City**. Shortly after this, they began a second town on the east side of Cherry Creek. They decided this would be a better location. They named their city **St. Charles**. Once they had chosen their spot, they left one of the men there to protect that area. The others returned to the Kansas Territorial legislature to get permission to build their new town."

"Why would they go to the Kansas Territory to get

permission for their town?" wondered Ed.

"The Pikes Peak area was a part of the Kansas Territory at this time. The Kansas Legislature made all of the important decisions about this area.

"The men who organized the town of St. Charles had hoped to make a lot of money by selling cabin sites within their town."

"Why would anyone pay for a cabin site when there was all kinds of free land all around them?" asked Nicole.

Sometimes miners built cabins to live in while they looked for gold.
(Credit: C.H.S.)

"Great question," praised Mr. Brown. "That is the same thing many of the men who were already out there were feeling, so they started a new town on the other side of Cherry Creek. They named it *Auraria*. Miners were not charged to live in the city.

"In November, a man named *General William Larimer* led a group of men into the area. They decided that they would take over the town of St. Charles. Since there was only one man living there, they took over the town and said it had been abandoned. They renamed the town *Denver City*."

"Why didn't they name it Larimer after the leader of the group?" asked Bryan.

"They chose to name the new town after the governor of the Kansas Territory. He was *General James W. Denver*," answered Mr. Brown.

The Word Spreads

"It didn't take long for many people to find out about the gold discoveries. As people traveled through this area, they would find out about the gold and tell other people they met. Newspapers would report about large nuggets of gold that could be picked up out of the streams. Some people even wrote books about it, encouraging people to go to the Pikes Peak area. During the winter of 1858-1859, there were three more discoveries of gold in this area.

"In January of 1859, *George A. Jackson* went up *Clear*

The city of Denver was named after James Denver, governor of the Kansas Territory.
(Credit: C.H.S.)

111

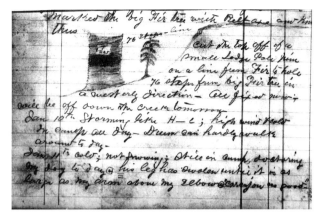

This page from George A. Jackson's diary tells where he found gold.
(Credit: C.H.S.)

John H. Gregory found gold near Gold Hill.
(Credit: C.H.S.)

"Pikes Peak or Bust" was written on the side of many wagons headed for the Pikes Peak Territory.
(Credit: C.H.S.)

Creek Canyon. He built fires to thaw the frozen ground. He melted snow in a tin cup to help find the gold. Even in these difficult conditions, he was able to find about ½ ounce of gold. He marked his spot so he knew where to return in the spring.

"That same month, six men found gold at the bottom of *Gold Hill*. Then, in April, *John H. Gregory* found gold. At this point in time, these men had not found very much gold, but it was enough to begin the *Pikes Peak Gold Rush*."

"Why did they call it the Pikes Peak Gold Rush?" asked Brink. "They weren't on Pikes Peak were they?"

"Good question," said Mr. Brown. "They were not on Pikes Peak, but they needed a name to tell people where they had discovered gold. Most people had heard about the famous Pikes Peak. They were in the same general area as Pikes Peak, so they called it the Pikes Peak Gold Rush. It wasn't long before over 100,000 people were on their way to this area.

"Most would not begin their journey until the spring of 1859 because they didn't want to travel in the winter. As a result, this group of prospectors were called the '*Fifty-Niners*.' Many of them had signs on their wagons that said '*Pikes Peak or Bust*.' "

"What does that mean?" asked Juan.

"It means they were determined to make it to Pikes Peak to get rich. Unfortunately, many of them busted. Out of the 100,000 prospectors, it is believed only about half of them ever made it to the Colorado gold fields."

"Why did only half of them make

it?" asked Ed.

"Some of them died from thirst, starvation, or disease along the way. Many got lost or their wagons broke down. Some became discouraged and returned home. Others were attacked by Plains Indians who were upset that all of these people were on their hunting grounds. Of the ones who reached the gold fields, only about half of them stayed very long. Panning for gold was very hard work and not very many men made much money."

Black Hawk. • Boulder
Golden. • Central City

Mining and Supply Towns

"New towns and settlements began to spring up all over the place. Some of these new settlements were **supply towns**. These were larger towns that provided supplies to many of the **mining towns** or camps.

"A group of men from Nebraska camped at the **Red Rocks** near the mouth of **Boulder Canyon**. They named their town **Boulder City**. West of the town of Denver, **Arapahoe City** and **Golden** were started. **Fountain City** was started south of the mouth of **Fountain Creek** . It was near the ruins of old Fort Pueblo. Another group started the town of **El Paso** near Pikes Peak. Later, other mining towns including **Central City, Black Hawk, Nevadaville**, and **Gregory Point** were started."

"I have never even heard of some of those towns," said Keith.

"Some of these early settlements became ghost towns. After all of the gold was found in that area, these towns were deserted and left to rot. Other towns went on to become important communities in Colorado."

Central City was sometimes called the richest square mile on earth. This picture shows Central City in the 1860s.
(Credit: C.H.S.)

Black Hawk was a mining town in early Colorado.
(Credit: C.H.S.)

113

Mining For Gold

Gold Pan

Sluice Box

Sluice boxes were often worked by several miners.
(Credit: C.H.S.)

Kelli's hand shot up in the air. Mr. Brown called on her.

"I know we have been talking a lot about mining for gold, but I am not sure I understand how they did it," Kelli said. "When they panned for gold what kept the gold from washing out of the pan with the sand?"

"They used a flat pan shaped like a big pie pan," Mr. Brown explained as he drew a picture on the board. "They scooped sand and gravel into the pan. Then they swished it around with water. The pan was moved around and around like they were stirring something. This motion swished the sand and gravel out of the pan. The gold was heavier. It fell to the bottom of the pan.

"At times they found tiny flecks of gold. These flecks were called **gold dust**. Sometimes they found larger pieces of gold called **nuggets**. These nuggets were often the size of rice or corn. Once in a while the nuggets were even bigger. Miners got really excited when they found a nugget. A nugget could be worth anywhere from $10 to $1,000."

"Boy, that sounds like a lot of work. Didn't they find easier ways to get the gold?" asked Adam.

"Panning was only used to find an area with gold," explained Mr. Brown. "Once they found it, they would build **sluice boxes**."

"What was a sluice box?" asked Kate.

"It was a long box that was placed on a slant," Mr. Brown explained as he drew another picture on the board. "Wooden bars were fastened to the bottom of the box. These bars were called **riffles.** Sand and gravel were shoveled into the

114

box. Water flowed over the riffles. This washed the sand and gravel out of the box. The gold was heavier. It sank to the bottom and was trapped against the bars or riffles.

"They sometimes placed a heavy liquid metal called **mercury** along the riffles. Gold would mix with mercury. This helped to trap the gold. Later they could separate the gold and the mercury. Groups of men would work together with one sluice box. Some sluice boxes were twelve feet long. Sluice boxes needed lots of water in order to work."

"What would they do if they weren't near water?" asked Nicole.

"Sometimes they would dig ditches or build a **flume**," answered Mr. Brown. "A flume was a long wooden box like a sluice box but without riffles. Ditches and flumes were used to bring water to the mining site. They could only do this if the area that was being mined was down hill from the water supply."

"What would they do if they didn't have enough water to use a sluice box?" asked Kelsey.

"They made **cradle rockers**," said Mr. Brown as he drew a picture.

"You mean like a baby's cradle?" asked Maria.

"As a matter of fact, that is probably where they got the idea. They made a wooden box about three feet long. Riffles were placed along the bottom of the box. They placed this box on rockers like those on a baby cradle. Another box with holes in the bottom was placed on top of the bigger box. This was called the **hopper**. Sand and gravel were shoveled into the hopper. Water was poured over it. The cradle was rocked back and forth. This washed the sand and gravel out of the hopper into the bottom box. Water flowed over the wooden bars, or riffles, and washed the sand out of the cradle. The heavier pieces of gold became stuck behind the bars."

"I thought that they dug tunnels into the side

Flume

Cradle Rocker

Cradle rockers were used to help find gold.
(Credit: Idaho Historical Society)

115

Hydraulic mining washed the hills and stream banks away.
(Credit: C.H.S.)

An arastra was used to crush the ore.
(Credit: Idaho Historical Society)

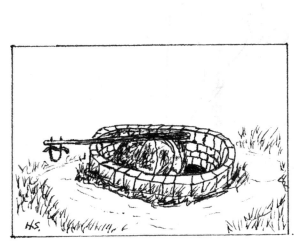

of a mountain to find gold," said Keith.

"We have been talking about finding gold that was on top of the ground or in stream beds," said Mr. Brown. "That is called **placer mining**. Once the gold that was near the surface had been found, men began digging into the earth. They hoped to find veins of gold. This was called **underground**, **hard rock**, or **lode mining**. Lode mining cost a lot of money. Many miners just left their mines because it cost too much to get the gold out."

"I saw a picture once of a man shooting a fire hose at a cliff," said Jessie. "They said that he was mining."

"When there was enough water, some miners did use pipes or hoses," said Mr. Brown. "The stream of water washed the dirt away. This was called **hydraulic mining**. This was much easier than breaking the soil up with a pick or shovel. A lot of hills and stream banks were ruined by this type of mining.

"Miners were really lucky when they found a **vein**. A vein was almost pure gold. It was unusual to find a vein. Usually they found **ore.** This was rock that had gold or precious metals in it. Ore had to be crushed in order to get the gold out of it. Miners crushed the ore in an **arastra**. This was a round hole lined with rocks. A dragstone was

Arastra

pulled around by a horse. This dragstone would crush the ore against the rocks. If there was plenty of water, the arastra might be run by water power.

"By 1865, they began building **stamp mills.** The stamp mills used heavy metal machines to crush the ore. They were expensive, but they did the job a lot better and faster than the arastras.

Stamp Mill

"Another thing they used were **ball mills**. These were round, hollow balls made out of iron. The miners placed the ore and some hard metal pellets inside the balls. They turned the balls on a shaft. The pellets hit the ore and broke it up into smaller pieces. The gold was then separated from the rock.

"The miners needed to find an easier way to separate the gold from the rock. Many different people came up with ideas. *Nathaniel Hill* traveled to Wales, Great Britian, to learn how they were able to process the gold. In Wales, he learned about smelting and in 1868 he opened his own smelting plant in Black Hawk. *The Boston and Colorado Smelter* was a success."

The Birth of a State

Nathaniel Hill opened a smelting plant in Blackhawk.

(Credit:

"Did everyone who came to Colorado come to mine for gold?" asked Keith.

"No, different people came for different reasons," replied Mr. Brown. "For example, explorers came to explore. The mountain men came to trap beaver. Traders came to trade. But, it was gold that brought enough people to Colorado so that it could become a state.

"The discovery of gold brought thousands of people to Colorado. They began to realize how many wonderful things there were in Colorado and began to settle here. Soon there were enough people that this area could take the first steps toward becoming a state."

"What did they have to do to become a state?" asked Lindsay.

"Good question, Lindsay," said Mr. Brown. Just then the bell rang. "We'll have to talk about that later. Let's see how quietly we can go outside for recess."

This was an early stamp mill that was built by John Gregory.
(Credit: C.H.S.)

117

What Did You Learn?

1. How did Denver get its name?
2. What was the nickname given to prospectors who came to Colorado in 1859?
3. What was the saying that many prospectors painted on their wagons as they headed to the gold fields of Colorado?
4. What heavy metal did they use to help trap the gold?
5. Name three ways they did placer mining.
6. What type of mining used stamp mills?
7. Explain how hydraulic mining was done.
8. How were flumes used?
9. What is ore?
10. How did the discovery of gold help make it possible for Colorado to become a state?

What Do You Think?

1. If you had lived back East in 1859, do you think you would have traveled to the Pikes Peak area to try to find gold? Why or why not?
2. How do you think the miners felt about taking gold and land that belonged to the Indians? Why?
3. If you were a placer miner what method would you use? Why?

Use Your Imagination

1. Pretend you are a miner. Describe what you think a typical day might be like.
2. You are a Ute Indian Chief in 1860. Tell how you feel about the miners coming onto your land.
3. Imagine that you are a prospector in early Colorado. You have just discovered a large vein of gold. What are you going to do? How will you spend your money? Write a story about this. It might be fun to make this a tall tale.

Chapter 9
War

It was a beautiful Monday morning. Mr. Brown's students were outside waiting for the first bell to ring. They talked excitedly about what they had done that weekend. Finally the bell rang. Mr. Brown let the students in and they began to settle into their seats.

Suddenly Yeong Se shouted out, "Hey Mr. Brown, someone has been into the things in my desk!"

"Someone has moved all of my stuff around!" exclaimed Abigail.

"Some of my stuff is missing," cried Keith.

"And my pencils are missing!" added Kelsey.

"I know," said Mr. Brown. "I needed some pencils and things so I just helped myself."

"But those were our things," said Kelsey. "Why would you just come and take our stuff?"

"How does this make you feel?" Mr. Brown asked.

"I don't think you should be able to just take our stuff," said Kevin.

"But I'm the teacher," said Mr. Brown with a shrug. "I can do what I want."

"You can't take things that don't belong to you," said Gania.

"Why would you do this?" asked Tim.

"I wanted you to see what it would feel like for someone to take your things."

"Why?" asked Maria.

"I just wanted you to know what the American Indians might have felt like. As we have seen, the trappers, traders, and early explorers usually got along with the Indians. The Indians were trading for items like metal tools and guns that made their lives easier. But as more and more settlers came into Colorado, many problems developed.

"We have been talking about some of the problems between the settlers and the Indians. The settlers had been taking over the American Indian's land. They had begun to settle on Indian hunting grounds. They were putting up fences. This was hard for the Indians to understand. They were becoming angry with the settlers. You became upset when you saw that someone had taken your things. Just think how angry you would feel if someone came in and tried to take your home away from you.

"The settlers were also bringing diseases like **cholera**. The Indians had never been exposed to these diseases, so it was very difficult for them. In one summer, nearly half of the Cheyenne died from cholera."

"I read that the settlers were also killing lots of the buffalo," Adam said. "They would just take the tongue and leave the meat to rot. I'll bet that made the Indians mad."

"You're right," agreed Mr. Brown. "As you know, the buffalo was important to the Indians. It was very hard for them to see the settlers waste this food. What else might have caused problems?"

"The miners were coming on to their land to search for gold," said Kate.

"Yes," Mr. Brown nodded. "The United States government had signed treaties with the Indians. They promised to give the Indians special areas to live called **reservations**. They said they would leave the Indians alone as long as they stayed on these reservations. At first this worked out fine. Then the government began to break their promises. The settlers would find out that there was gold on the reservation, or that there was good farmland. They would get the government to make the reservation smaller so they could have this good land. Pretty soon the Indian reservations were getting smaller and smaller. Indians were having a hard time finding food. The government promised to bring them food. Once again these promises were broken."

"How could they do that to the Indians?" asked Bryan. "Why was the government always breaking its promises?"

"It was a terrible thing," continued Mr. Brown. "The Indians wondered the same thing. They could not trust the settlers. It is sad to say, they began to hate all settlers. They were angry and wanted to get back some of the things that had been taken away from them. They needed food and supplies. Some of them began to kill in order to get what they needed. Indians who had fought against each other were now working together to fight the settlers. The settlers became afraid of all Indians. Some would shoot any Indian they saw. Everyone was scared and many wanted revenge. What happened is that many innocent people lost their lives."

"I didn't know that the settlers had been so mean to the Indians," said Brink.

"There were a lot of broken promises," said Mr. Brown. "The settlers and the government did not understand the Indians, and the Indians did not understand them. Many people began to fight to get what they wanted. Just like in any war, there were bad things happening on both sides. Let me tell you about some of these conflicts."

120

Plains Indians

"At first, the Plains Indians tried to get along with the new settlers. They believed the promises made to them by the United States government. They had been told the plains would be their hunting ground forever. When the city of Denver was being built, many of the Indians camped nearby so they could watch. Most of them became friends with the settlers.

"As time passed, the buffalo were quickly being killed by people traveling west. There were fewer and fewer buffalo for the Indians to hunt. The Indians were becoming angry because they could not get enough food. Some of them began to raid ranches. They would kill or steal cattle and horses. Some would attack wagon trains headed west. Sometimes pioneers would be killed during these raids. Most of the attacks were done by just a few young warriors.

"During this time, there was a war going on back East between the northern and southern sections of the United States. Most of the soldiers were called away from Colorado to fight in the *Civil War*, so they were not there to protect the settlers. *John Evans* was the governor of the Colorado Territory at this time. He ordered all of the Indians to move to army forts. He told them that if they gave up all of their weapons, he would provide them with food. He then said that any Indian who did not move to the army forts would be considered hostile, or unfriendly. Settlers were given permission to shoot any 'hostile' Indians.

"Winter was approaching. The Indians knew it would be hard to find food in the winter, so most of the Indians agreed to move to the forts. They camped near *Fort Lyon* by *Sand Creek*. They thought they would be safe because they had done what they had been asked. They were wrong."

John Evans ordered the Indians to move to army forts.
(Credit: C.H.S.)

Fort Lyon

This picture of Fort Lyon was painted by Robert Lindneux.
(Credit: C.H.S.)

121

Colonel Chivington led the Sand Creek Massacre.
(Credit: C.H.S.)

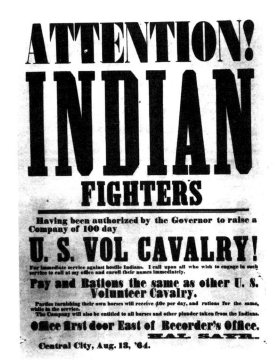

Posters were used to recruit soldiers.
(Credit: C.H.S.)

"Many of the settlers did not believe the Indians wanted to live in peace. They believed that all Indians should be feared and punished.

"*John Chivington* was a minister and a soldier. He asked men to join him to fight the Indians. Chivington wanted a big battle to punish the Arapaho and the Cheyenne. He and his men traveled to Sand Creek."

"Isn't that where the Indians were camped?" asked Joe.

"That's right," answered Mr. Brown. "On the morning of November 29, 1864, Chivington and his men attacked the Indian camp. It is said that Chivington told his men not to take any prisoners. The Indians were caught off guard. Most did not have any weapons. *Black Kettle*, the chief of the village, stood waving an American flag."

"Why was he waving the flag?" wondered Lindsay.

"He was hoping the soldiers would realize that they were making a mistake," said Mr. Brown. "It didn't do any good. It is said the soldiers killed between 200-500 Indians. Different people say different things. No one really knows for sure how many people were killed, but most of them were women, children, and older men."

"Did all of the Indians die?" asked Paul.

"No," replied Mr. Brown. "Most of the ones who survived were sent to a reservation in present day Oklahoma. Some of the younger warriors did not go. They began to attack settlers. They burned stagecoach stations and

Robert Lindneux painted this picture of the Sand Creek Massacre.
(Credit: C.H.S.)

towns. Telegraph lines were torn down. In 1865, the Civil War ended. The Colorado soldiers who had been fighting in the Civil War returned home. They continued to chase and fight the warriors who were still fighting for their way of life. Eventually, these Indians were either killed or went to the reservation."

"What happened to Black Kettle?" wondered Kelli.

"Amazingly, Black Kettle was not killed in the Sand Creek Massacre. He even continued to try to work for peace between the settlers and the Indians. About four years later, he was killed when a cavalry troop lead by *George Armstrong Custer* attacked his village. Black Kettle's village was attacked even though they were camped on Indian land with the white flag and American flag flying to show that they were peaceful."

"That is terrible," exclaimed Zach. "I can't believe the soldiers attacked the Indians like that. They just wanted to live in peace."

"It was a terrible thing," agreed Mr. Brown.

"What happened to Chivington after the Sand Creek

Black Kettle worked for peace between the settlers and the Indians.
(Credit: C.H.S.)

Massacre?" asked Chelsea.

"It is amazing to know that many of the settlers considered Chivington a hero," answered Mr. Brown. "The United States government finally looked into the Sand Creek tragedy and found Chivington guilty of leading a massacre."

"Was he punished for what he did?" asked Michael.

"Not really, although he did pay a price for what he did. At one point in time, many people thought he would become one of the first congressman of Colorado. His punishment was that he couldn't be involved in politics or in Colorado's fight for statehood. He was also forced to resign from the Colorado militia. He moved around and worked in different jobs until he died from cancer in 1892."

Ouray, center of picture, met with leaders from the United States government to try and make peace.
(Credit: C.H.S.)

Ute Indians

"The Ute Indians had problems similar to the Plains Indians. Settlers wanted to farm and raise cattle on the Utes' hunting grounds. Prospectors moved onto Indian land to mine for gold. The Ute decided they had a couple of choices. They could give up their land to the settlers, but then they would not have any hunting grounds. How would they be able to get food? Another choice was to learn how to farm or ranch.

"*Ouray* was an important Ute leader. His name means arrow. His mother was an Apache. His father was an Uncompahgre Ute. Ouray was brought up by a Spanish family, so he learned to speak English and Spanish, as well as his native tongue.

"Ouray felt that the Ute Indians needed to change or the soldiers would come and fight. He started a farm and raised sheep. He even moved into a house that the U.S. government built for him.

"Many of the Ute did not agree with Ouray. They did

Captain Jack was a Ute leader who did not want to change his way of life.
(Credit: C.H.S.)

not want to change their ways. **Captain Jack** and **Douglas** were two Ute leaders who felt that way. They lived near the **White River** in western Colorado. There was an Indian agency at White River. An agent of the United States government was sent there to teach the Indians how to become farmers. His name was **Nathan Meeker**. For a while the Utes listened to Mr. Meeker. The Ute children went to a school that Mr. Meeker began.

Nathan Meeker was killed after he plowed up an Indian race track.
(Credit: C.H.S.)

"Horse racing was very important to the Utes. Mr. Meeker did not approve of the horse racing. One day, he plowed up one of the race tracks to plant crops. The Indians were very angry. They attacked and killed Meeker and all of the men working there. The women and children, including Meeker's wife and daughter, were taken as prisoners."

"What happened to the prisoners?" asked Jessie.

"The Utes released them after a few days," responded Mr. Brown. "The soldiers asked Ouray to help make peace. Ouray did his best to keep peace and to protect the rights of the Indians. Douglas, one of the leaders of the Meeker Massacre, was the only one punished. He was put in jail for a short time. Most of the other Utes moved to a reservation in Utah."

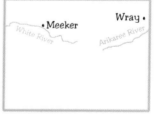

Douglas, on the left, was one of the leaders of the Meeker Massacre.
(Credit: C.H.S.)

"What happened to Ouray?" asked Nicole.

"He died just before his people moved to the reservation," answered Mr. Brown.

Beecher Island

"In 1868, one thousand Cheyenne, Sioux, and Arapaho trapped 50 troops on **Beecher Island** in the **Arikaree River**. This was near the present day town of **Wray**. For nine days they attacked the soldiers. Eventually, more soldiers arrived and saved the troops that were trapped on the island."

Robert Lindneux painted this picture of the battle on Beecher Island.
(Credit: C.H.S.)

125

Summit Springs

"Although most of the Indians had moved to reservations, there was a group of Indians who refused to go. They were called 'dog soldiers'. The leader of this group was called **Tall Bull**. In 1869, soldiers killed Tall Bull in a fight at **Summit Springs**. He was the last war chief. This was one of the last battles in Colorado."

The page above was from a Summit Springs sketch book.
(Credit: C.H.S.)

Ads like this appeared in some newspapers.
(Credit: C.H.S.)

Reservations

"What happened to all of the Indians living in Colorado?" asked Juan.

"All of the Indians were required to leave Colorado except for a small part of the southwestern part of the state. By 1881, almost all of the American Indians in Colorado were living on reservations. Over time, the reservations became smaller. The Indians could no longer hunt buffalo where they wanted. The land on the reservations was poor, so it was difficult to grow crops. The government had promised they would supply the Indians with food and clothing. Once again the government did not provide enough supplies. Children were forced to go to missionary schools. Here they were taught the 'American way.' They were not allowed to keep their own traditions and customs.

"Today there are over 22,000 American Indians living in Colorado. There are two reservations in the southwestern part of the state. They are the **Ute Mountain Ute Reservation** and the **Southern Ute Reservation.** Many Northern Ute Indians live in Utah.

"Around 4,000 Arapaho Indians live on the **Wind River Reservation** in Wyoming, and many more live in Oklahoma.

About 3,000 Northern Cheyenne live on a reservation at Lame Deer, Montana. Around 5,000 Southern Cheyenne do not live on reservations. They live in towns near Concho, Oklahoma. There are Indians from many tribes around the country that choose not to live on the reservations. Many live in other places so they can find better jobs and schools.

In August of 1881, Ute Indians left Colorado for a reservation in Utah.
(Credit: C.H.S.)

"Many American Indians who are living on reservations today face lots of problems. A lot of them are having a hard time finding jobs. When they do get jobs, many times the money they earn is barely enough to survive. Places like the Ute Mountain Ute Reservation have recently opened casinos to help create new jobs and to bring more money into the reservation.

"Even though they face many problems, American Indians work hard to hold on to their heritage. For example, many of them are learning to read and write in their native tongue. They also try to keep many of their beliefs and rituals alive. Each year, Cheyenne from around the country gather in Oklahoma for a Sacred Arrows Ceremony."

"I think it is really sad how the settlers treated the Indians," said Lindsay. "I think they should have been nice to them. Then the Indians would have been nice to the settlers."

"That is a good point," agreed Mr. Brown. "If settlers had tried to live with and learn from the Indians rather than pushing them aside, Colorado would be an even better place today. Can you imagine what it would be like if we had learned to live like them? What if we took better care of our earth? Maybe we can still learn from them today. Maybe it is not too late.

"Speaking of taking care of things, I believe I have some of your stuff," said Mr. Brown as he handed back the things he had taken from their desks. "Thank you for being such good sports about this."

What Did You Learn?

1. What is a reservation?
2. Why were the reservations getting smaller?
3. Name two reasons why the Indian wars happened.
4. Why did some of the Plains Indians get mad enough to attack ranches and wagon trains?
5. What did the governor of Colorado promise to give the Indians if they gave up all of their weapons?
6. What happened to Black Kettle after the Sand Creek Massacre?
7. What happened to John Chivington after the Sand Creek Massacre?
8. Who was the governor of Colorado during the conflicts between the Indians and the settlers?
9. What happened to the Indian agent Nathan Meeker?
10. Who was the Ute leader who tried to make peace with the settlers?

What Do You Think?

1. What do you think can be learned from the conflicts between the settlers and the Indians?
2. What do you think you would have done if you had been Black Kettle?
3. What do you think you would have done if you had been John Chivington?
4. What do you think could have been done to prevent the wars?
5. What if the settlers had tried to live like the Indians instead of trying to make them change? How do you think things would have been different?

Use Your Imagination

1. Pretend you are a young Indian during the Indian Wars. Describe what you think a day in your life would have been like.
2. Describe what it might have been like to be on a wagon train that was under attack.
3. Describe what you think Colorado would be like today if the settlers had never come here. How would the lives of the Indians be different?

Chapter 10
Territory to Statehood

Mr. Brown's class was returning from P.E. one day. As they entered the room, they noticed the words "Pikes Peak or Bust" written on the chalkboard.

"We've already studied the gold rush," said Lindsay. "Why do you have that saying on the board Mr. Brown?"

" 'Pikes Peak or Bust' was the cry of many people who headed west in hopes of finding gold," answered Mr. Brown. "This saying was also printed on many wagons that were headed to what was known as Pikes Peak **Territory**. The Pikes Peak area was really not a territory. If you remember, we said that this area was part of the Kansas Territory."

"What do you mean by territory, Mr. Brown?" asked Erin.

"A territory is part of the United States. It is not a state yet, but it has a governor and other people to help run the area. The president of the United States chooses these leaders. Once there are enough people living in a territory, they can ask to become a state.

"The northeastern part of what is now Colorado was part of the *Nebraska Territory*. The Western Slope of Colorado was part of *Utah Territory*. The part that was south of the *Arkansas River* was in *New Mexico Territory*. The middle eastern section of Colorado was a part of the *Kansas Territory*. To make things even more complicated, most of this area was land that, by treaty, belonged to the Indians.

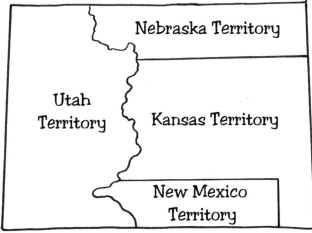

At one time Colorado was part of four different territories.

"The miners and prospectors were so far away from the capital of the Kansas Territory that they decided to set up their own rules. They formed what were called **mining districts**. They wrote their own constitutions and elected their own officers. The laws they wrote told how large a mining claim could be and what a person had to do in order to make a claim. The secretary, or recorder, for each mining district kept a record book listing all the claims and who owned each one.

"The people, who settled in the valleys and began farms, organized **claim clubs**. These claim clubs were very similar to the mining districts used by the miners. The people in each area would write a **constitution**. A constitution is a paper that lists the laws and beliefs of a group of people in a certain area. The settlers also chose a group of people to help settle arguments. Sometimes farmers argued over land and water rights. Since the farmers were concerned about Indian attacks, the club also banded together for safety. The settlers wanted the federal government to survey the land and then sell it at public auction. Those who were already settled would then have the first right to purchase it.

"These claim clubs and mining districts worked fine for a while, but the people really wanted to create a separate territory. The territory would be smaller and the government would be closer and better able to help enforce the laws. Several bills were presented to Congress in 1858 and early 1859 to make Colorado a separate territory. All of these bills failed.

"In April of 1859, a group of miners from several different communities decided that the Pikes Peak area needed to become a state. They chose the name *Jefferson* for the new state. About this same time, many of the miners became discouraged. They were not finding the large amounts of gold they expected. There were a large number of 'go backs' or people who were returning home. This made the population of this area too small to be considered for a state. The men who were trying to form the state of Jefferson gave up and returned to their mines.

"In August, these same men met again. This time they wrote a state constitution. Then they asked all the people of the area to decide if they wanted to become a state or a territory. Most of the people who voted asked that this area become a territory. Once again Congress turned them down.

"The people went ahead and formed *Jefferson Territory.* Legislators were elected and they met to make the laws. They tried to pass a tax that would make it possible to run the territory. Since it wasn't an official territory, many of the miners refused to pay the tax. The legislators had no money to run the territory so this plan failed.

"People kept trying to get Congress to make the Pikes Peak area an official territory of the United States. Many people did not like the name Jefferson. They felt that only President Washington should be honored in this way. Several other names were suggested. Pretty soon the name Colorado became the most popular of these names, but once again, Congress refused to make this area an official territory.

"In 1860 Kansas became a state. The western border of the new state of Kansas no longer included the land that is now part of Colorado. It was finally decided that Colorado could now become a territory. On February 28, 1861, before he left office, President *James Buchanan* signed the bill to make Colorado an official territory."

"Was the *Colorado Territory* just the land in the Pikes Peak area?" asked Kelli.

"No, the borders of the Colorado Territory had the same shape as the state of Colorado today," Mr. Brown answered.

"*President Abraham Lincoln* appointed *William Gilpin* as the first governor of the Colorado Territory. The legislature was elected by the people. *Hiram P. Bennet* was elected to represent the Colorado Territory in Washington, D.C. Bennet had the nickname of '*Garden Seed*' because he promised to send all the voters free packages of vegetable seeds after the election.

William Gilpin was the first governor of the Colorado Territory. *(Credit: C.H.S.)*

"The federal government became so involved in the *Civil War* that little attention was paid to the new Colorado Territory. Most of the soldiers in Colorado were sent East to fight in this war. Governor Gilpin was afraid that Southern troops might try to capture the Colorado Territory. He wanted to have an army to protect the new territory. He issued **drafts** to pay for all the equipment he needed for his army."

"What were drafts?" asked Kevin.

"Drafts were like an I.O.U. They were pieces of paper that were used like money or a check. These drafts said that the federal government would pay the money owed. Governor Gilpin told people that President Lincoln had given him permission to write the drafts. Mr. Lincoln had not given permission and the government refused to pay the drafts. This

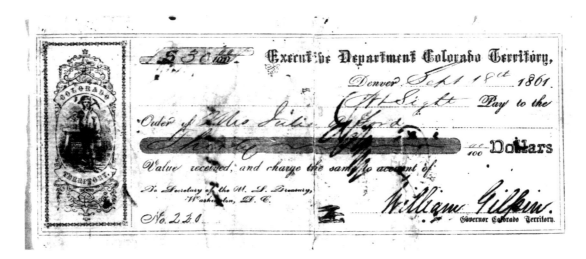

This draft for $30 was signed by Governor Gilpin.
(Credit: C.H.S.)

General Sibley wanted to capture Colorado for the South.
(Credit: C.H.S.)

made lots of people really mad at Governor Gilpin. They felt that the governor had lied to them. They began trying to get a new governor."

"Did the army formed by Governor Gilpin ever have to fight in the Civil War?" asked Ed.

"Yes they did," said Mr. Brown. "*General Henry H. Sibley*, a southern general, began moving his army across the southwestern desert. He wanted to claim the Colorado Territory for the south. His army started into Colorado over *Glorieta Pass*. The *Colorado Volunteers* led by *John Chivington*, rappelled down the canyon walls into the pass and surprised the enemy's supply train. They destroyed all the supplies. This made it impossible for General Sibley to continue into Colorado. This defeat kept Colorado land and the gold that was being mined here from being claimed by the South. Chivington was called a hero by many."

"Wasn't he the same guy who led the *Sand Creek Massacre*?" asked Adam.

"Yes he was," answered Mr. Brown, "but you must remember we are talking about 1862. The Sand Creek Massacre happened three years later.

"Most of the people in Colorado were happy that the Colorado Territory had an army to protect them. That did not keep them from being angry at the way Governor Gilpin had raised the money for this army. The people kept asking for a new governor.

"In April of 1862, President Lincoln appointed a new governor. *John Evans* was chosen to take William Gilpin's place. He arrived in the Colorado Territory in May of 1862. He discovered that there were several problems here. As you may remember, during this time, the Indians and the settlers were not getting along. Governor Evans had the job of trying to bring peace to the territory. Another big problem facing the Colorado Territory was the need for an easier and more rapid form of transportation."

Sometimes the train would have to stop while a herd of buffalo crossed the tracks. *(Credit: C.H.S.)*

Early Transportation

Railroads

"Governor Evans had high hopes that the **transcontinental railroad** would come through Colorado on the way to the Pacific. He knew that the railroad would be important to the growth of Colorado. The railroad would be able to bring in large machinery for mining and logging. It would also make it easier for new settlers to get to Colorado."

"I thought that *John Gunnison* had said it would be too hard to build a railroad because of the high mountains and deep snow," said Paul.

"He did," said Mr. Brown. "The people who were planning the transcontinental railroad had read his reports. They found an easier way to get across the mountains further north. In 1867, the *Union Pacific* laid tracks across the Wyoming prairie.

"People in Colorado were upset that the railroad was not coming through Colorado. Railroads helped people get around quicker, easier, and cheaper. They also helped companies be able to ship their products and supplies easier. This helped to improve prices.

"The people decided to build connecting, or **feeder tracks**, from

#1 Union Pacific Railroad
#2 Santa Fe Railroad
#3 Kansas to Denver Feeder Line
#4 Cheyenne to Denver Feeder Line

133

Golden ••Denver

Colorado •
Springs

the Union Pacific tracks in Wyoming south into Colorado. ***William A. H. Loveland*** was a mine owner who wanted to see a railroad line come into ***Golden***. Governor Evans was trying to get the railroad to come to ***Denver***. The ***Colorado Central Railroad*** began building a line to run from Cheyenne to Golden since it was closer to the mines.

"Denver was the capital of the territory and had a lot more people than Golden. The people in Denver were upset that the railroad was being built to Golden and not Denver. They began working to get a railroad into Denver. In June of 1870, a track from Cheyenne to Denver was completed. To help celebrate the completion of this railroad, a silver spike was used as the final spike.

"Another line was started in Kansas to go to Denver. It was completed in August of 1870. Denver now had two railroad lines. The line from Cheyenne to Golden still was not completed. Golden did not get a railroad from the north until 1877.

"In 1871, ***General William J. Palmer*** began building the line that would be known as the ***Denver and Rio Grande***. This railroad would have a narrow gauge track. The rails would be only three feet apart. The narrow gauge would make it possible for the train to go around steep curves more easily. The track would run north to south from Denver to El Paso, Texas. By autumn of that year, the railroad tracks reached from Denver to the place where ***Colorado Springs*** would later be built.

The Denver and Rio Grande Railroad crossed LaVeta Pass.
(Credit: C.H.S.)

"The ***Santa Fe Railroad*** ran from Topeka, Kansas, across the southeast corner of Colorado, and over the Raton Pass to Santa Fe, New Mexico.

"Several other railroad lines were built on the eastern slope between 1870 and 1880," continued Mr. Brown. "Other parts of the Colorado Territory were not so lucky. They had wagon roads and trails that pack trains could use. It was not until 1875 that a wagon road was finished across the mountains. Stagecoaches and freight wagons could now get from one side of the mountains to the other.

It wasn't until 1928 that the famous *Moffat Tunnel* was finally completed and the first train rolled through the mountains. This cut off 175 miles between Denver and *Winter Park*. By 1934 tracks were completed to allow trains to travel between Denver and Salt Lake City."

Winter Park • •Denver

Stagecoaches

"The **stagecoach** was an early form of travel. Before the railroad, stagecoaches were the fastest form of transportation. The stagecoach carried passengers, mail, gold, and silver. These coaches were pulled by four to six horses. It was not very pleasant to travel by stagecoach. It was crowded, dirty, and smelly. The coach would travel at full speed over bumpy roads. In summer, the trip was hot and dusty. In the winter, it was cold and damp. Many times the stagecoach could not even travel in the winter.

"The stagecoach would stop at a **swing station** every 12 miles to get fresh horses and drivers. The travelers could get a meal such as bread, beans, bacon and black coffee. About every 50 miles they would stop at a home station for the night. In 1859, it cost about $100 to ride the stagecoach across the plains. It took about 11 days. Traveling by wagon over this same distance would take about 5 weeks.

"Some of the roads in Colorado were so steep that the stagecoaches had to drag huge logs on the ground behind them when going down a hill. These logs would act as a brake to keep the coach from going downhill too fast."

"I saw a movie one time where a stagecoach was robbed. Did that happen a lot?" asked Michael.

"Yes indeed," nodded Mr. Brown. "The driver and guard always had to watch out for robbers who wanted the gold and mail the stage carried. They also had to watch out for Indian attacks. It was not always safe to travel by stagecoach."

Traveling by stagecoach was not easy.
(Credit: C.H.S.)

135

Before roads, pack trains were the only way to get supplies to the mines.
(Credit: C.H.S.)

"Before Colorado had wagon roads, goods and supplies were taken to the mines by strings of pack horses or mules. One **pack train** might have as many as 100 animals. These animals could carry very large loads as heavy as 250 to 400 pounds.

"**Freight wagons** were also used for carrying heavy loads. They often hitched three wagons together. The first was usually the largest. The middle one was a little smaller. The last one was the smallest. These wagons were pulled by one or two dozen horses, mules, or oxen. If the animals were oxen, the driver was called a **bullwhacker**. A **muleskinner** would drive the mules. The wagons could only go where there were roads. It was an expensive way to carry things. It was also very slow.

"Some say that more than one hundred million pounds of freight were brought into Colorado by wagons in 1865. Each year after that, the number of pounds of freight shipped into Colorado got larger."

Freight wagons carried heavy loads over steep roads.
(Credit: C.H.S.)

136

Roads

"One of the most famous roads in the world cut across the southeast corner of Colorado. It was called the **Santa Fe Trail.** Freight wagons, pack trains, and wagon trains carrying cargo and pioneers traveled over this famous road.

"Many of the roads were so bad that people began building private toll roads. The builders would charge a **toll**, or a fee, for travelers to use this road. **Otto Mears** built several roads and became famous for his work. He built one road over the area where part of Colorado's **Million Dollar Highway** now runs."

"I heard that the gravel Mears put on his road had gold in it," said Keith. "That is why the road was named the 'Million Dollar Highway.'"

"That's one of the stories that has often been told. I believe it really got its name in the early 1920s. They rebuilt a section of this road from **Ouray** to the top of **Red Mountain Pass**. One of the workers realized the cost for this section would be a million dollars. He began to call it the 'Million Dollar Highway.' The name has stuck with this road.

"Some of the highest roads in the world are in Colorado. **Mount Evans Highway** runs to the top of **Mount Evans**. **Trail Ridge Road** in **Rocky Mountain National Park** rises to 12,183 feet."

Otto Mears helped open western Colorado with his roads and trains.
(Credit: C.H.S.)

• Ouray
// Red Mountain
Pass

Trail Ridge Road in Rocky Mountain National Park is one of the highest roads in the world.
(Credit: C.H.S.)

137

Communication

William Byers published Colorado's first real newspaper.
(Credit: C.H.S.)

"For a long time, newspapers and the **Pony Express** were the main ways for people in the territory to get news. Newspapers were brought in from far away places. Often the news might be a month or more old. Some of the mining towns had news sheets that came out from time to time. They were not regular and none lasted for very long.

"The first real newspaper in Colorado was the **Rocky Mountain News** published by **William Byers**. His first paper hit the streets on April 23, 1859. This was just twenty minutes before **John Merrick's Cherry Creek Pioneer** was finished. Every city and town wanted their own newspaper and by 1867, there were five daily, eight weekly and two monthly newspapers in the Colorado Territory.

"**Julesburg** was the only Pony Express stop in Colorado. This helped to bring daily news from the East. In 1863, the first telegraph line began operations between Julesburg and **Denver**. The **telegraph** was quicker and cheaper, so it soon replaced the Pony Express. In 1879 the **telephone** was brought to Denver. A few months later it was installed in **Leadville** and other cities."

Julesburg•

•Denver

Leadville•

The Rocky Mountain News printing room was a very busy place.
(Credit: C.H.S.)

Schools

"Most of the early settlers in Colorado were miners. Many did not bring their families with them until later. In October of 1859, Denver had its first classroom. It was a private school taught by *'Professor' O.J. Goldrick*. There were 13 students the first day. Each student paid three dollars a month to come to the school. Most students paid their tuition in gold dust. Very few students went beyond 8th grade.

"Even though the students paid to go to school, this was not enough for the teachers to make a living. Most of the 'professors' found that they had to find ways to make extra money.

"Soon other private schools were opened in Denver. *Miss Indiana Sopris* was the first woman to teach in Colorado. She opened a private school in Denver in 1860. There were also private schools in *Mount Vernon* and *Golden* around this same time. The first school building in Colorado was built in *Boulder* in 1860.

"In 1861, the legislature started public schools. Soon there were schools in most of the mining camps. This made it easier for the miners to bring their families to the mining camps.

"In 1863, the Methodist Church started building the *Denver Seminary*. The following year they changed the name to the *Colorado Seminary*. In 1880, this school became the *University of Denver*. The *University of Colorado* in Boulder opened its doors to the first class of 44 students in 1877. In Colorado Springs, the Congregationalists founded *Colorado College* in 1874. That same year the legislature funded the beginning of the *School of Mines* in Golden. The *College of Agriculture* in *Fort Collins* opened its doors in 1879. There were nineteen students in the first class. This is now *Colorado State University*. Many new people were drawn to Colorado because of these schools of higher education."

"Professor" Goldrick opened the first private school in Denver.
(Credit: C.H.S.)

Miss Sopris was the first woman to teach in Colorado.
(Credit: C.H.S.)

The first school house in Colorado was built in Boulder in 1860.
(Credit: C.H.S.)

Fort Collins.

Boulder.
Golden.

Colorado
Springs.

Reverend John Kehler started the Church of St. Johns in the Wilderness.
(Credit: C.H.S.)

Churches

"Preachers came to Colorado right after the miners. Most of these men traveled from mining camp to mining camp holding services.

"The church building with its steeple or tower and bell became the pride of almost every community. It gave the people a feeling that their community would be permanent. The church building reminded the people of their town back home. It made the men feel as if they could bring their families to a place that felt more like home.

"Many of the religious services held in the mining towns were led by men who had been leaders in their churches back home. In April of 1859, the Methodist Episcopal Church started a mission. They sent **Reverend W.H. Goode** and **Jacob Adriance** as missionaries. By August they had started **Trinity Church** in Denver.

"In 1860, **The Reverend Mr. H.J. Kehler** was sent by the Episcopal church. He started the **Church of St. Johns in the Wilderness** in Denver. There were also Presbyterian services in Denver that summer. A Jewish group started the **Temple Emanuel** congregation in that same year. Shortly after this, both the Baptists and Congregationalists started churches.

"Two priests, **Father Joseph P. Machebeuf** and **Father J.B. Raverdy** came to Denver from Santa Fe. They arrived in October of 1860. With very hard work they were able to finish their Catholic Church in time for services on Christmas Day, 1860."

Statehood

"From 1861 to 1876, the Colorado Territory had eight different governors."

"Why did they have so many governors?" asked Zach.

"Some of them were not very honest and used their office to get money and land for themselves. There were some who were much more interested in their own needs than the needs of the territory.

"All during this time, there were some men who were

Bishop Machebeuf helped build the first Catholic church in Colorado.
(Credit: C.H.S.)

working for statehood and some who wanted Colorado to remain a territory. There were several **constitutional conventions** held during this time. These were meetings where the people would try to decide what the laws would be for Colorado. These constitutions were presented to the U. S. Congress. Each time they were turned down. One reason given was that Colorado would not let African-Americans vote. This was against the federal civil rights laws that were passed after the Civil War.

"On March 3, 1875, the U.S. Congress finally approved Colorado's request to become a state. *John Long Routt* who was the territorial governor at that time was chosen to be the first governor of the state of Colorado.

"Another constitutional convention was called. One decision that they had great difficulty making was whether or not to let women vote. The women really wanted the right to vote. If the men writing the constitution had decided to do this, Colorado would have been the first state to allow women to vote. They decided not to include this in their constitution. In 1893, Colorado became the second state to allow women to vote. Governor Routt's wife, Eliza, was the first woman to register to vote in Colorado.

"The voters of Colorado approved the new constitution on July 1, 1876. On **August 1, 1876**, *President Rutherford Hayes* signed the bill that made Colorado the **38ᵗʰ state**. That was the same year the United States celebrated its **centennial**."

"What is a centennial, Mr. Brown?" asked Juan.

"A centennial is the celebration of a 100 year anniversary. The United States celebrated the centennial of the signing of the Declaration of Independence in 1876. Since Colorado gained statehood the same year, it was nicknamed *'The Centennial State'*, " Mr. Brown said. "This was an exciting time for the people in Colorado. There were lots of parties to celebrate the fact that Colorado had finally become a state.

"I think we should celebrate too. I have a special party planned for this afternoon. I made a cake and decorated it to make it look like a map of Colorado. I also brought some punch. So, would you like to celebrate Colorado's statehood?"

The class cheered.

What Did You Learn?

1. What is a territory?
2. Who was the first governor of the Colorado Territory?
3. What was the first name chosen for the state of Colorado?
4. Who signed the bill to make Colorado a territory? Who signed the bill to make Colorado a state?
5. Before there were wagon roads, how did the supplies get to the mines?
6. Why was early transportation in Colorado so difficult?
7. Why was the railroad so important to Colorado?
8. What was the name of the first real newspaper in Colorado?
9. When did the first telegraph come to Colorado?
10. When did Colorado become a state?
11. When did the first telephone come to Denver?
12. Why is Colorado called the "Centennial State?"

What Do You Think?

1. What do you think it would have been like to live in Colorado before it became a state?
2. What do you think the early schools in Colorado were like? Do you think you would have liked to go to school back when Colorado was a territory? Why or why not?

Use Your Imagination

1. Imagine you have just traveled by stagecoach for one week. Describe what your trip was like.
2. Pretend you lived in one of the early towns in Colorado. Write about what it was like the first day the telegraph came to your town.

Chapter 11
Industries of Colorado

The students were just finishing a lesson in science. Mr. Brown asked them to clear off their desks and get ready for Colorado history.

"I thought we were all finished with Colorado history," said Jessie.

"Why would you think that?" questioned Mr. Brown.

"We celebrated statehood last time," replied Jessie. "Isn't that the end?"

"Colorado became a state over 125 years ago. A lot has happened since then. Unfortunately, we won't be able to learn about everything, but we will have time to study about a few more things. First we will talk about some of the **industries** of Colorado."

"What are industries?" asked Zach.

"They are things like farming, manufacturing, and ranching that provide jobs for many Coloradans," explained Mr. Brown. "We will talk about some of the main industries in Colorado. Let's start off with one that we have already talked about a little."

Aspen • •Leadville

Mining

"One of the first industries to begin in Colorado was mining. We already know how important mining was to Colorado. It brought enough people here for us to become a state. Let's talk a little bit about what happened to mining after Colorado became a state.

"In 1878, a new metal caused a stir in Colorado. Does anyone know what it was?"

"I'll bet it was silver," stated Joe.

"You are right," replied Mr. Brown. "*Leadville* and *Aspen* were two big silver mining towns. The

Leadville in the winter of 1897-98.
(Credit: C.H.S.)

143

Aspen around 1889
(Credit: C.H.S.)

Bob Womack found gold
in a cow pasture.
(Credit: C.H.S.)

largest silver nugget ever found was in Aspen. It was found in 1894, and weighed 1,840 pounds. By 1880, Colorado was the richest mining state in the United States. Colorado was sometimes called the '*Silver State*.'

"Lots of silver was mined. As a matter of fact, too much silver was mined, so the silver prices dropped. There were not very many uses for silver. Some countries had stopped using silver to make coins. Silver was not used very much in jewelry. In 1893, the silver market crashed. Many miners lost their jobs and many mine owners lost all of their money.

"During the time that silver mining was going bad, a second gold rush began. In 1890, a cowboy named **Bob Womack** found gold in a cow pasture. Mr. Womack sold his claim for about $300. Too bad he didn't hold on to it. Over a half a billion dollars in gold was mined from this pasture.

"The town of **Cripple Creek** began near this gold field. By 1900, Cripple Creek was the second largest gold mining area in the world.

"Coal mining also played an important role in the development of our state. The settlers needed fuel. They were chopping down so many trees, that trees became scarce. The price of wood rose quickly. Settlers were looking for other sources of fuel. In the **Denver** and **Boulder** areas, coal was found as early as 1859. Settlers would just back up their wagons and chip the coal right in. Soon men claimed the right to mine this coal. This was the beginning of Colorado's coal industry.

"When the railroad came to this area, the demand for coal really increased. Trains used coal for fuel. They could also transport the coal to other places. Over time the railroad companies came to own most of Colorado's coal mines. **Trinidad** and **Walsenburg** are important areas for coal."

Walsenburg
(Credit: C.H.S.)

"By this time, most of the miners worked for a company. They often worked ten hour days. They were only paid $3-$4 a day. A lot of work was done by hand. Candles were used for light. It was hard, dangerous work. Mines could fill up with dust and gas which could cause an explosion.

"Many miners lived in what was called a **company town**."

"What is that?" asked Abigail.

"A company town was owned by the same company that owned the mine. The miners would live in houses that were owned by the company. All of the teachers, doctors, and people who worked in the town were chosen and paid for by the company. The company would even choose what newspapers the miners would be able to read. When the miners were paid, many times it was in **scrip**. Scrip was a piece of paper that could be used to purchase supplies, but only at the company store. It wasn't good anywhere else.

"Many times the company didn't have much concern for the safety and welfare of the miners. Around the 1890s, the miners began to form **unions**. This was a group that fought for the rights of the mine workers. They asked for safer working conditions and higher wages.

"When the mining companies did not agree to do what the union asked, the workers might **strike**, or not work. Tension began to build between the miners and the mining companies. There were many violent strikes and sometimes people were killed. Finally in the fall of 1913, something happened that began to change things.

Company town of Primero
(Credit: C.H.S.)

Colorado Fuel and Iron Company Store
(Credit: C.H.S.)

Sometimes strikers marched to protest the way the company treated them.
(Credit: C.H.S.)

145

Coal miners and their families lived in
tents during the strike.
(Credit: C.H.S.)

Checking the tent city after the fire
(Credit: C.H.S.)

Governor Ammons called
out the National Guard.
(Credit: C.H.S.)

J.D. Rockefeller owned
Colorado Fuel and Iron
Company.
(Credit: C.H.S.)

Josephine Roche tried to
help the miners.
(Credit: C.H.S.)

"It was called the **Ludlow Massacre**. Coal miners who worked in southern Colorado went on strike for more than six months. During this time, they were forced to leave the company houses. The miners moved into tents. In April of 1914, *Governor Elias Ammons* called in the National Guard. The soldiers tried to make the miners and their families leave the area where they were camped. When the 900 men, women and children refused to go, a scuffle broke out. During the fighting, the tent city caught on fire. Two women and 11 children were killed when they tried to hide in a cellar beneath a tent."

"How did they die?" interrupted Bryan.

"They died from breathing the smoke from the fire," continued Mr. Brown. "Six men also died during the fighting. When news of this event got out, people in the nation were shocked. They couldn't believe this had happened.

"*John D. Rockefeller* owned the most powerful mining company in Colorado. It was called the *Colorado Fuel and Iron Company*. He began to make some changes, but he still did not allow the men to form unions. The strikes continued.

"In 1927, a young woman showed that you could treat workers with respect and still earn a profit. *Josephine Roche* inherited her father's holdings in the *Rocky Mountain Fuel Company*. She had always felt sorry for the mine workers. She worked hard to improve working conditions and to raise the miners' wages. This company did very well. After this, things began to slowly improve for the mine workers."

"Is mining still important to Colorado today?" asked Yeong Se.

"Mining has continued to play a big role in the development of Colorado," explained Mr. Brown. "In the early 1900s, oil was becoming more important. Oil was called 'black gold.' Cars had been invented and the oil was used to make gasoline. After World War II the demand for oil increased.

Climax Mine is the world's largest underground molybdenum mine.
(Credit: C.H.S.)

"Coal, oil, and natural gas are the state's main mining products today. Gold, silver, and **uranium** are also important. Uranium is used for nuclear energy. The first atom bomb was created from uranium mined here in Colorado.

"**Molybdenum** is also mined in Colorado. Nearly three fourths of the world's molybdenum comes from our state. It is used to make steel harder. The ***Climax Mine*** is the world's largest underground molybdenum mine, but it is not open right now. The only molybdenum mine in Colorado that is operating at this time is the ***Henderson Mine*** in the mountains west of Denver."

• Climax

Agriculture

"Mining, Colorado's first industry, created the need for other industries. When miners first came to Colorado, stores were few and far between. Miners had to bring their own food with them. They also had to hunt for food. This took so much time, they did not have as much time to look for gold. As a result, some people made a living out of supplying the miners with food. At first, food was brought in from many miles away. It was difficult to do this since there were not many roads. Finally some men began to grow food closer to the mines. Miners paid large amounts of money for food grown by the farmers."

"I'll bet the farmers got really rich!" exclaimed Kelli.

147

Many farmers on the eastern plains of Colorado built their homes out of sod.
(Credit: C.H.S.)

"Many of them did very well for a while," explained Mr. Brown. "When the ore began to run out in the mountains, many miners left to look for gold somewhere else. Since miners were their main market, many farmers went broke. A few were able to last until transportation improved. Then farmers were able to sell their goods to other parts of the country.

"The government wanted people to settle on the land. They passed the **Homestead Act**. This gave settlers 160 acres of land. The settlers had to live on the land for five years and farm it, in order to own the land.

"The Colorado plains were covered with a thick layer of sod, or grass. The farmers had to plow up the sod to get to the rich soil below. Their nickname became the '*sodbusters*.' Since there were not very many trees to build houses, the farmers built their houses out of dried sod. The walls would be as much as two feet thick. This kept the house cool in the summer and warm in the winter.

"In the 1930s, our nation was going through the ***Great Depression***. That was a time when many people were out of work and had lost much of their savings. It was a difficult time, but something happened to make things even worse. A big **drought** caused many farmers to lose their land. A drought is when there is very little rainfall. Water would be scarce, which made it difficult to grow crops. Since the grass that used to hold the soil in place had been plowed up, strong winds would carry the top soil great distances. This area became known as the ***Dust Bowl***.

"Eventually things began to get better for the farmers in Colorado, but they still faced many hardships. Grasshoppers would sometimes come in and destroy their crops in only a few hours. Prairie fires could wipe out their hard work. Every few years there would be a severe drought.

Irrigation helps make it possible to grow crops throughout Colorado.
(Credit: C.H.S.)

"It wouldn't be possible to raise crops in a large part of the state without **irrigation**. Who remembers what irrigation is?"

"That is when you bring water from some place else to water crops," stated Gania.

"You're right," noted Mr. Brown. "Over the years, farmers found that irrigation had to be used to grow crops in lots of areas. Many dams were built to store water. Today, most farmers use pipes and sprinkler systems to irrigate their crops. Some places in Colorado get enough rainfall to raise crops without irrigation. This is called **dry farming**.

"In the early days many irrigation ditches were dug. In 1852, a group of Hispanic settlers dug the *San Luis People's Ditch*. This is Colorado's oldest irrigation canal in continuous use.

"These irrigation ditches carried water from a river or lake to the farms. Farmers made furrows or tiny ditches in their fields. They would then let water from the big ditches run into the tiny ditches in their fields. This would water their crops.

"It was expensive digging canals and irrigation systems. Many farmers formed colony settlements and worked together. They combined their money and skills to help make their farms successful. By working together, it also helped the farmers to not be so lonely.

Horace Greeley wrote about Colorado in his New York newspaper.
(Credit: C.H.S.)

"The best known **colony settlement** became the town of *Greeley*. It was named after *Horace Greeley*. He was a newspaper man who wrote about his colony settlement in his New York newspaper. His writings encouraged many people to head west. Even though colony settlements were successful, most of the eastern plains were settled by individual farmers.

"Over the years, more and more canals were built. All of these canals took water from the rivers. The farmers along the river did not have as much water as they used to have. At one point in time, the state of Kansas filed a law suit against the state of Colorado. They claimed that Coloradans used too much water out of the *Arkansas River.*

The town of Greeley around 1870-1871
(Credit: C.H.S.)

149

People in Kansas did not have enough water for their crops. A judge ruled that since the Arkansas River began in Colorado, that Colorado farmers had the first right to that water.

"In 1922, a group of people from seven states along the Colorado River met to discuss water rights. They went against what the judge had ruled and decided that each state should have an equal claim to the water.

"There were many places in Colorado that were too far away from a good source of water to get water easily. Millions of dollars have been spent trying to get water from one place to another. For example, in the early 1900s the federal, state, and local governments began building dams and tunnels to deliver water to where it was needed. Water was taken from the mountains where few people live to more heavily populated areas.

"In 1909 the **Gunnison Tunnel** was opened. This water tunnel is 30,600 feet long, 11 feet wide and 13 feet high. The whole tunnel was lined with concrete. Water from the **Gunnison River** is sent under Vernal Mesa to be used on the farms and ranches near **Montrose** and **Delta**.

"Water from the **Roaring Fork River** is piped under **Independence Pass** to the Arkansas River to help irrigate the eastern plains of Colorado. Another project takes water from the **Aspen** area and sends it to **Leadville, Salida, Cañon City, Pueblo** and several cities in the **San Luis Valley**. These are only a few of the important water tunnels in Colorado.

"There have been a lot of angry words about how much water should be sent from one area to another. People in the dry areas need lots of water so they can farm and have water in their homes. People who live where there is lots of water are afraid that all of their water will be taken from them. There are also people who feel that these tunnels and dams will harm the environment and kill the fish. Water rights are still an important issue facing many of the states.

"Farmers in Colorado grow fruits like pears, plums, peaches, and cherries. They also produce corn, hay, grains, wheat, potatoes, and lettuce.

The Gunnison Tunnel opened in 1909.
(Credit: C.H.S.)

"**Weld County** is one of the largest agricultural counties in the country. Nearly all of the potatoes that are grown there are made into potato chips.

"Onions are Colorado's biggest small-farm vegetable crop. Colorado ranks 3rd in the nation for the number of onions it produces.

"Juan, you said your uncle grew cantaloupes at **Rocky Ford**. That area is famous for its cantaloupes. It is even called the '**Nation's Melon Capital**.'

"Denver is often called the '**Carnation Capital**'. Over 100 million carnations are raised there each year.

"Once the crops are grown, Colorado has factories that get the food ready to go to market. For example, **Longmont Foods** processes foods like turkey bologna and turkey hot dogs. Some places in Colorado process sugar beets into sugar."

Farm workers get the cantaloupe ready to go to market.
(Credit: C.H.S.)

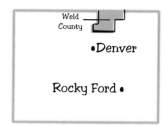

Cattle and Sheep

"The first herd of cattle came to Colorado from Texas in 1859. The cattlemen drove the cattle along trails into Colorado. These trails needed to be within reach of water and have grassy areas every 5-6 miles. It was also important that there not be timbered areas or fences along the trail. The cattlemen would camp every 10-15 miles. A herd of cattle was usually between 2,000-3,000 cattle. Ten to fifteen men would be hired to drive the cattle along the trail.

"One of the more famous of these trails was the

In the fall cattle were rounded up and taken to market.
(Credit: Idaho Historical Society)

----- Goodnight-Loving Trail

Goodnight-Loving Trail. Two men named Charles Goodnight and Oliver Loving decided to bring cattle into Colorado. They knew Colorado was a mining area with lots of money. It also had good grazing areas. They sold many of their cattle to *John Iliff*, who was sometimes called the '*Cattle King of the Plains.*' He became very rich selling beef to the miners and railroad workers.

"Once they reached Colorado, the cattle were allowed to roam and graze on the lush green grasses of the Colorado prairies. There were no fences to separate the animals. They all grazed in the same meadows. This was called the **open range**. In the fall, the cattle were gathered together. Does anyone know what this was called?"

"Was it a **roundup**?" asked Abigail.

"That's right," Mr. Brown said. "The cattle were rounded up and taken to market. Some were taken by railroad to cities far away. The cattle were sold and the money was sent to the ranchers."

"How did they know which rancher got the money?" asked Erin.

"That is why **brands** were so important," explained Mr. Brown. "Each rancher had a different brand. Every spring, the new calves were branded by the cowboys."

"How did they know which brand to put on which calf?" wondered Ed.

Cattle were branded each spring.
(Credit: Idaho Historical Society)

"The baby calves stayed close to their mothers," Mr. Brown explained. "The cowboys would brand the babies with the same brand as the mother. When the cows were taken to market, a person would keep track of how many cows had each brand. The money was sent to those ranchers.

"Since the winters were mild in the valleys, the ranchers did not need to have a place to keep their livestock. This was great. It did not cost the ranchers anything to feed or house the animals. These men became rich very quickly. Cattlemen liked the open range.

"Then things started to change. Homesteaders began to settle and farm on what had been open range. They built fences around their property. A barbed wire machine was built in 1874. This machine allowed farmers to fence their land a lot cheaper. There was not as much land available for grazing cattle. The

152

cattlemen blamed the farmers for many of their troubles.

"Around this same time, something else happened that affected the cattle industry. Quarantine laws were passed by the government. These laws said that cattle could not cross the state line into Colorado until they had been held for 90 days. During this time, they would check to make sure that the cattle were not sick. They didn't want any diseases brought into Colorado. Another thing the cattlemen could do was to have a veterinarian check the cattle for disease. If the veterinarian said it was all right, the cattle could come into Colorado.

Sheep have been raised in Colorado for a long time.
(Credit: Idaho Historical Society)

"Since the cattle industry was such a profitable business, many men brought cattle into Colorado to feed on the open range. Pretty soon, there were too many cattle and not enough grass for them to eat. This along with some very severe blizzards in the mid-1880s, caused the decline of the cattle industry.

"Sheepherders had been raising sheep in Colorado before any cattle were being raised here. As the need for wool and the meat from the sheep increased, more and more sheep were brought into Colorado. They could not be turned loose like the cattle. They had to be herded and watched over. Sheepherders used dogs to help them herd the sheep.

"The cattlemen did not like having sheep on what they considered to be their land. They said that the sheep ate the grass too low to the ground. Some cattlemen believed that cattle would not eat or drink where sheep had eaten or had been drinking. They said that the sheep left a bad odor from oil glands in their hooves. This is not true.

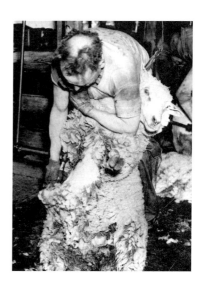

"The other thing was that many cattlemen were prejudiced against the sheepherders and looked down on them. This caused bad feelings between the sheepherders and the cattlemen. There were shootings, bombings, and poisonings. These were known as the ***Range Wars***.

The wool from sheep is used to make many different products.
(Credit: Idaho Historical Society)

"The open range only lasted about 20 years. Good grassland became harder and harder to find. The ranchers learned that they needed to grow hay to feed their animals during the long winters. There were some very long, cold

153

Today, many cattle and sheep are fed in feed lots like this one near Greeley.
(Credit: C.H.S.)

winters. The ranchers lost a large number of their cattle. Cattlemen and sheepherders were not able to make as much money as they did at first."

"Do they still raise a lot of cattle and sheep here in Colorado?" asked Kevin.

"Yes, cattle and sheep are still important to Colorado today," answered Mr. Brown. "Most cattle do not roam like they used to. Many are fed in feed lots. They eat grain instead of grass. ***Monfort*** near ***Greeley*** is the largest cattle feeder in the United States. Colorado also has more sheep and lambs in feedlots than any other state."

Tourism

"We have many wonderful places to visit. People come from all over the world to enjoy Colorado. They spend money in our state. This is a part of another industry called tourism. Tourism is one of the top ten industries in Colorado.

"Many tourists enjoy our beautiful mountains, lakes, and rivers. They like to fish, hike, camp, hunt, and many other things. In the winter, people like to go skiing at places like ***Aspen, Breckenridge, Vail,*** and ***Crested Butte.*** More than 10 million people ski on our slopes each year. The state's first rope tow was put in at ***Berthoud Pass*** in 1937.

"In the summer, rafting down the beautiful rivers is a popular sport. People also like to visit ***Rocky Mountain National Park*** and ***Pikes Peak***. There are many things to see and do in Colorado."

Rafting on the Colorado River can be a fun and exciting adventure.

Manufacturing

"The Front Range has become a center for technology. Companies like ***IBM*** and ***Hewlett Packard*** are important to Colorado. Colorado ranks in the top 10 for making computers.

"A lot of scientific instruments are produced in our state. Medical supplies such as heart monitors and artificial blood are produced in Colorado.

"Waterpiks, which are used to help you clean your teeth,

are also produced in our state.

"**Coors Brewing Company** is the world's largest brewery. Only the state of Texas produces more beer than our state.

"One of the largest steel plants in the United States is **Colorado Fuel and Iron Corporation** in **Pueblo**. Pueblo is sometimes called the '**Pittsburgh of the West**' because a large amount of steel is produced in both of these places."

Other Industries

"There are many other important industries in Colorado. There are more federal agencies located in our state than anywhere else in the United States except Washington, D.C. Denver is often called '**Little Washington.**' The **Denver Mint** makes 5 billion coins every year. If you see a 'D' stamped on a coin, you know it was made here in Colorado.

"Colorado has become a major defense center. In 1957, Canada and the United States began a program to guard against Russian air attacks. It is called **NORAD**. This stands for North American Aerospace Defense Command. It is located near Colorado Springs. It is 1,200 feet underground inside **Cheyenne Mountain**. They can use radar to show if an air attack is coming toward the United States.

"Also near the city of Colorado Springs is the **Air Force Academy**. This is where Air Force cadets are trained."

"Are these the only industries in Colorado?" questioned Michael.

"Gosh, no," replied Mr. Brown. "We have only had time to talk about a few of them. People in Colorado work in many different types of jobs. The natural resources of Colorado have made many of these industries possible.

"Another important resource in Colorado is the people. Some of these people have become very famous. Next time, we will find out about a few of them. Right now, let's clear our desks and get ready for math."

The U.S. Mint in Denver makes billions of coins each year.
(Credit: C.H.S.)

•Denver

Colorado Springs
•

•Pueblo

NORAD is located in Cheyenne Mountain near Colorado Springs.
(Credit: C.H.S.)

The United States Air Force Academy is near Colorado Springs.
(Credit: C.H.S.)

What Did You Learn?

1. What is a union? Why were unions formed?
2. What happened in 1893 that affected many silver miners in Colorado?
3. Name three minerals still mined in Colorado today.
4. How was the Homestead Act important to Colorado?
5. Why is irrigation important to Colorado?
6. Name three crops grown in Colorado.
7. Why did the cattlemen want to get rid of the sheepherders?
8. What is an open range?
9. Why are brands important?
10. What Colorado city is sometimes called the "Pittsburgh of the West?"
11. What is NORAD?
12. Name five things that tourists like to do or places they like to visit in Colorado.

What Do You Think?

1. Do you think a company town was good or bad for the miners? Explain your answer.
2. What is your favorite place to visit in Colorado? Why?
3. What are some industries that are important to your area?

Use Your Imagination

1. You have a job as a travel agent. Tell someone why they should come to Colorado for their vacation. What should they see?
2. Write a story about how things would have been different if gold had not been discovered in Colorado. What do you think would have brought people here to settle?
3. Pretend you have come to Colorado to be a farmer. Tell about your life as a sodbuster. What crops did you raise? What hardships did you have? Were you able to make it as a farmer?
4. You are a miner. Convince the mine owner that you should get more pay.

Chapter 12
Famous People in Colorado

Mr. Brown walked into the classroom. He told the class that he had two very special visitors. Just then, a man and a woman walked in. The woman was dressed in a beautiful long dress with a fancy feather hat. The man had a large bushy mustache and wore a fancy suit with a long coat. Mr. Brown had to hold his hand up for silence. The excited voices of the class quickly died down.

"I would like to introduce you to **Horace Austin Warner Tabor** and his wife **Baby Doe**," said Mr. Brown. "They have agreed to come from the past to tell us about their lives. Let's find out more about them. I would like to begin with you, Mr. Tabor. Would you please tell us about your life in early Colorado?"

Horace Tabor was known as the "Silver King of the Rockies."
(Credit: C.H.S.)

"I'd be happy to. Back in 1859, I came to Colorado because I had heard about gold in the Pikes Peak area. I tried prospecting, but soon gave it up. I became a shopkeeper. After many years in Colorado, I finally began to do pretty well. I was even elected the mayor of **Leadville** and the treasurer of **Lake County** in 1878.

"As a shopkeeper, I had a habit of **grubstaking** many miners. I would give them food and supplies. They would then agree to split their findings with me. One time this really paid off. In May of 1878, two miners, that I had grubstaked, struck it rich. They found the **Little Pittsburgh Mine**. I was able to sell my part of the mine for one million dollars."

"Wow, that was quite a bit of money. What did you do with it?" asked Mr. Brown.

"I used some of the money to buy new mines. One of them was called the **Matchless Mine**. This was a very good

Baby Doe Tabor
(Credit: C.H.S.)

Baby Doe
TABOR

1884

and

1934

— • —

Matchless
Mine,

Leadville,
Colo.

Leadville •

mine and we earned lots of money from it. I also built the ***Tabor Opera House*** in Leadville and the ***Tabor Grand Opera House*** in ***Denver***."

"Baby Doe, when did you and Horace meet?" asked Mr. Brown.

"We met in 1882. When we were married, it was quite an event. Even the President of the United States, ***Chester Arthur***, was there. Horace gave me a beautiful diamond necklace. I was told that it was the one that Queen Isabella from Spain had sold to help pay for Christopher Columbus' first voyage to the New World. Horace always bought me nice things. He even bought me a lovely mansion in Denver."

"You two did live a very glamorous lifestyle. Then something happened in 1893, that changed your lives forever. Would you please tell us about that?" said Mr. Brown.

"Yes, the price of silver went way down. We lost everything."

"That must have been very difficult for both of you. I appreciate you coming back here to tell us about your life in early Colorado," said Mr. Brown. The man and the woman walked out of the classroom as the class cheered.

"What ever happened to them?" asked Kelsey.

"Mr. Tabor died penniless in a fancy room at the Brown Hotel in Denver in 1899. As he was dying, he told Baby Doe to hold on to the Matchless Mine, because it would be worth

158

something someday. She went up to the mine and lived in a shack until her death in 1935."

"How did she die?" asked Gania.

"They found her frozen to death after a big blizzard," answered Mr. Brown. "I hope you have learned a few things about the Tabors. I am glad that Mrs. Johnson and Mr. Brigham were able to come in and help me with this presentation today."

"That was fun, Mr. Brown," said Yeong Se. "I felt like I really met the Tabors."

"I'm glad you thought it was fun," said Mr. Brown. "There are many interesting people who have done a lot for Colorado. This next two weeks we are going to have time to learn about some of them. You will work in groups of two or three. I would like each group to choose a famous person. Learn all you can about that person, and then you will do a presentation for the rest of the class."

"Do we have to dress up like our person?" asked Michael.

"No, but you may if you wish," Mr. Brown stated. "I would like you to use your imagination and see how you can make your report interesting. I have several books in the back of the classroom. I am sure that Mrs. Allred, the librarian, will help you find others. First, you will have to decide who your report will be about. I want each group to choose a different person."

Two weeks later Mr. Brown handed out a list. "This is the order in which we will do our reports," he stated. "We will start with the first group on Monday."

Scott Carpenter

The following Monday when the students arrived, they saw a cone-shaped space capsule made out of cardboard in the front of the room. AURORA 7 was printed on the side. Suddenly Yeong Se stepped out from behind the space capsule. Tim came in from the back of the classroom. He was wearing a sports jacket and a hat with a sign that said "PRESS."

Tim walked up to Yeong Se and said, "*Mr. Scott Carpenter*, if you have a minute, I would like to interview you for the *Eagle Eye Review.*"

"Certainly," he answered.

"When were you born?" asked Tim.

Scott Carpenter was both an astronaut and an aquanaut.
(Courtesy: National Aeronautics and Space Administration)

Boulder .

"I was born in 1925 in **Boulder**, Colorado."

"I understand that you began your career as a U.S. Navy test pilot," said Tim.

"That is correct. I was chosen as one of the original *Mercury 7* astronauts in 1959. On May 24, 1962, I became the second American to orbit the earth. As a matter of fact, this is the space capsule I was in when I orbited the earth 3 times," he said as he pointed to the AURORA 7.

"What did you do after that?" asked Tim.

"I took a leave of absence from NASA and became a part of the Navy's Man-in-the-Sea Project. I spent 30 days living and working on the ocean floor. We were 205 feet under the water."

"From what I understand, that makes you the only human to work both in outer space and under the ocean."

"That's correct," he replied. "I was an astronaut and an aquanaut. Later I returned to NASA where I was an Executive Assistant to the Director of the Manned Space-Flight Center. I helped to design the Apollo Lunar Landing Module."

"Is it true that in 1967 you returned to the Navy to work with an underwater project?"

"Yes, I was Director of Aquanaut Operations during the Sealab III experiment."

"Are you still doing that?" asked Tim.

"No, I have been doing some writing and speaking. I have also helped on ocean and space projects."

"Thank you very much for your time, Mr. Carpenter. I enjoyed talking with you very much."

Tim and Yeong Se went back to their seats as the class clapped.

160

Florence Sabin

Erin and Gania came into the room carrying a rocking chair. Erin wore a long dress and bonnet. She sat down in the rocking chair and Gania sat at her feet. Gania looked up at Erin and said, "Grandma, you said you knew someone who worked really hard to help fight diseases, like tuberculosis, in Colorado. Would you tell me about her?"

"Yes," Erin answered. "Her name was **Florence Sabin.** Florence was born in **Central City** on November 9, 1871. Her father worked in the mines in Central City. Florence had an older sister named Mary whom she loved very much. Two younger brothers died as infants, and her mother died from an illness when Florence was only seven years old."

"What happened to Florence after her mother died?" asked Gania.

"Since her father was so busy in the mines, Florence and Mary were sent to a boarding school. The following year they were sent to live with their aunt and uncle. While she was living there, Florence learned to play the piano. She loved playing the piano and wanted to become a concert pianist when she grew up.

Dr. Florence Sabin worked hard for good health for all.
(Credit: C.H.S.)

"Later, Florence and her sister went to live with their grandparents. Her grandmother kept telling Florence about the long line of doctors in her family. Her grandmother said that it was too bad that she was not a boy because she would make a good doctor. This remark made Florence angry. She decided that she wanted to be a doctor. When her grandmother died, Florence went back to live with her aunt and uncle.

"Florence worked very hard in school. When she went to college, she found out that she was one of the smartest girls in her class. She loved school and spent all of her time studying. She took lots of science classes and really enjoyed being in the lab. She decided to go into research. She learned everything she could about the human body. Florence studied the human brain and made a model that taught doctors things they did not know. She studied white blood cells and learned that they help the body to fight disease. Dr. Sabin taught classes all over the world. She won many awards for her research. When Dr. Sabin was 67, she was forced to retire."

"What did she do then?" asked Gania.

"She moved back to Denver and lived with her sister. When she was 73, **Governor John Vivian** appointed her head of the health committee of a state planning commission. Florence was thrilled to be working again.

"She found out that Colorado had some of the worst health conditions in the country. Dr. Sabin wanted to find out how to improve conditions in Colorado. The water in Colorado was dirty. The milk carried diseases. People were eating meat from sick cattle. Vegetables that were grown in Colorado were not good to eat. Trash piled up on the streets.

"Dr. Sabin made a list of these problems and suggested ways to make things better. This list was called the **Sabin Health Bills**. Almost all of Dr. Sabin's bills became laws. After that, things in Colorado began to change. Colorado now had better standards for milk and meat. The water was cleaner and safer.

"Dr. Sabin also suggested that the state should give free X-rays."

"Why did she want the state to give free X-rays?" asked Gania.

"**Tuberculosis** was a big problem in Colorado. This was because many people with tuberculosis had moved here. They were told that Colorado's clean air would help to cure them. Tuberculosis is a disease of the lungs. An X-ray could catch the disease sooner, so there was a better chance for the doctors to help cure the patient. Hundreds of thousands of X-rays were given. Over 4,000 people were found to have tuberculosis. Once this program was started, the tuberculosis rate was cut in half.

"Dr. Sabin loved baseball. She watched whenever she could. She died of a heart attack while watching the 1953 World Series."

"Dr. Sabin was a wonderful person," said Gania. "I can't believe all of the things she did. She never gave up even when the going got tough."

"You're right," replied Erin. "Dr. Sabin once said that women can have whatever they are willing to work for. She accomplished a lot in the areas of medicine and science as well as in the area of women's rights. A statue of her represents Colorado in Statuary Hall in the United States Capitol."

"I think she is a good person to represent our state," said Gania.

"Me too," agreed Erin.

The girls stopped and turned toward the class. Everyone clapped. "Great job!" exclaimed Mr. Brown.

John Elway

Michael and Keith came jogging into the classroom from the coatroom. They were dressed in Denver Bronco football uniforms. Michael was carrying a football and yelled, "Hey Keith, catch!"

Michael tossed the ball. Keith caught it and shouted, "Touchdown!"

The class began to cheer.

"That was a great catch, Keith," said Michael. "I still can't believe that game my folks recorded. It was so cool to watch when the Denver Broncos beat the Falcons in the Super Bowl."

"It was a great game," said Keith. "*John Elway* was awesome. He is one of the best quarterbacks ever. Did you know that he is the first quarterback to start in five Super Bowls?"

"He sure is awesome," agreed Michael. "I was looking up some things on the Internet after the game. Look at what I found. John Elway was born in Port Angeles, Washington, on June 28, 1960. When John was in the fourth grade he played his first football game. He ran for six touchdowns in the first half of the game."

"Hey, look," said Keith. "It says his favorite sport to watch and play is golf."

"And his favorite subject in school was math," said Michael. "That's one of my favorite

Englewood •

John Elway led the Denver Broncos to a 1998 Super Bowl Championship.
(Credit: C.H.S.)

subjects, too. I also thought this was neat. He ate the same meal before every game."

"What was it?" wondered Keith.

"French toast, eggs, and hash browns," answered Michael.

"He says that the best advice he ever received was from his dad," noted Keith. "His dad told him to treat other people the way he wanted to be treated. That is what my parents always tell me."

"Did you know that John was a really good baseball player also?" asked Michael. "In 1982 John played on the farm team for the New York Yankees. He had a .318 batting average and he was credited with 24 runs in 42 games. In 1983 he was the first draft pick chosen by the Baltimore Colts football team. He did not want to play for the Colts. He knew he could play baseball if he did not get on a football team he wanted to play for. Finally, the **Denver Broncos** worked out a trade for John Elway.

"John was voted Denver's Most Valuable Offensive Player six times. He was the NFL's most valuable player in 1987. He was also chosen as the AFC Offensive Player of the Year in 1993.

"John retired after his team won their second straight Super Bowl in 1999. He was inducted into the Football Hall of Fame in 2004."

The boys looked at Mr. Brown to let him know they were done.

"Great job, boys," said Mr. Brown. "John Elway was a super athlete. He sure helped to give the Denver Broncos a special place in football history."

Federico Peña

Juan and Brink walked up to the front of the classroom. Juan sat down at a desk in the front of the room and pretended he was working. Brink walked over to him and began to talk.

"Hey, Juan, what are you up to?"

"Oh, I am working on my project for the school cultural fair. I am supposed to do a project on a Hispanic person who has had an influence in the development of Colorado. I thought I would choose **Federico Peña**."

"That is a good choice," said Brink. "Wasn't he Denver's first Hispanic mayor?"

"Yes, he was," answered Juan. "I have been doing some research and have found out some interesting things about him. Would you like to hear some of them?"

"Sure," replied Brink. "What have you learned?"

"Federico Peña was born in Laredo, Texas, in 1947. He was the third of six children. When he grew up, he went to the University of Texas and earned his law degree.

"After this, he moved to Colorado and began to practice law. He was elected to the state legislature in 1979, and served four years there. After that he was elected as Denver's mayor. He was mayor for 8 years.

"In 1993, **President Bill Clinton** chose him to be the Secretary of Transportation. He was the first Hispanic American to head that department. In 1997, he was chosen by President Clinton to be the head of the Energy Department. In 1998, he resigned this position to spend more time with his family. He is back working in Denver."

Federico Peña was mayor of Denver for 8 years.
(Credit: C.H.S.)

"Wow, it sounds like he is a very important person," said Brink.

"He has done a lot for Colorado and the United States," continued Juan. "He helped make it so Colorado could build **Denver International Airport**. He has received all kinds of honors from many different organizations."

"Is Mr. Peña married?" asked Brink.

"He is married and has two children," answered Juan.

"That is really interesting, Juan. Thanks for sharing that with me. I have to run now. Good luck with your project."

Lon Chaney, Sr.

As the boys headed back to their seats, Abigail entered the classroom through the back door. Everyone in the class was surprised to see her dressed as Quasimodo from the *Hunchback of Notre Dame*. She was followed by Bryan who was dressed as the *Phantom of the Opera*.

"Good afternoon, ladies and gentlemen," began Abigail. "We are here today to tell you about the '**Man of a Thousand Faces**'."

"His name was **Lon Chaney, Sr.**," continued Bryan. "Mr. Chaney was born on April 1, 1883, in Colorado Springs. Both of his parents were profoundly deaf. This means they could hear hardly anything at all. Mr. Chaney had to communicate with them without words. Some people say that is what attracted him to the theater. As a young man, he worked as a stagehand, scenery painter, and sometimes played small parts at the Colorado Springs Opera House."

"Around 1900, Mr. Chaney and his brother began to tour with a stage company," added Abigail. "From 1913-1917 he made over 70 short and feature films. He became a master of makeup. He played starring roles in movies such as the *Hunchback of Notre Dame* and the *Phantom of the Opera*. He was well known for his horror films, but also played many other parts."

"Mr. Chaney died of cancer in 1930," concluded Bryan. "He was only 47 years old. Most of the movies he made were silent movies. He only made one talking movie. If he had lived, he probably would have starred in the first sound version of *Dracula*. His son, Lon Chaney, Jr., also starred in many movies."

"I wish I could have met Mr. Chaney in person. It would have been fun to meet the 'Man of a Thousand Faces,'" concluded Abigail.

Jack Dempsey

Kevin and Joe entered the classroom. They sat down at a table in the front of the room.

"Good evening, ladies and gentlemen," began Joe. "We would like to welcome you to this boxing match tonight. In the ring will be **Jack Dempsey.** He will be defending his heavyweight title once again. Who do you think will win tonight, Kevin?"

"I think Jack Dempsey is a sure winner. He didn't get the nickname '**Manassa Mauler**' for nothing," said Kevin.

"How did he get that name anyway?" asked Joe.

"Mr. Dempsey was born in Manassa, Colorado, in 1895," explained Kevin. "His real name was **William Harrison Dempsey**. When he started fighting, he was very aggressive. This earned him the

Jack Dempsy was nicknamed the "Manassa Mauler." *(Credit: C.H.S.)*

nickname the 'Manassa Mauler'."

"That is interesting. What else can you tell us about our world heavyweight boxing champion?" asked Joe.

"I guess as a child, he lived a very hard life. His family had to move a lot. Mr. Dempsey worked hard all his life. He was even a **mucker** in the mines in Colorado."

"A mucker? What is that?" asked Joe.

"A mucker was someone who shoveled the dirt from the mines. It was hard and miserable work. Mr. Dempsey would move from place to place trying to make his place as a fighter. He would travel the rails in the dead of winter. He wouldn't be inside the train where it was nice and warm. He would be hanging underneath the cars holding on for dear life. He could not afford to pay the fare, so this was the only place he could ride without getting caught. It was his determination and his hard life that have helped Mr. Dempsey to be where he is today."

"Wow, Kevin. That is hard to believe. I guess I'll be rooting for Jack Dempsey also. He is truly a fighter," said Joe.

"It looks like the fight is ready to begin. Thanks for that background on Jack Dempsey."

Clara Brown shared all she had with others.
(Credit: C.H.S.)

The boys stood up. Joe said, "Jack Dempsey was the world heavyweight boxing champion from 1919-1926. He fought in 69 professional fights. He knocked out his opponent in 47 of those fights. Mr. Dempsey lost his heavyweight title in 1926 to *Gene Tunney*. He died in 1983."

"Thank you boys," said Mr. Brown. "Great job."

Aunt Clara Brown

Chelsea, Lindsay, and Kelli came to the front of the room. "Our person is *Aunt Clara Brown*," Chelsea said. "We are going to do a play. I will be the narrator, Lindsay will be Aunt Clara and Kelli will play the part of Becky Johnson. Becky is Aunt Clara's best friend. They met in Leavenworth, Kansas, in 1857 when Aunt Clara was about 57 years old. Our play opens with Aunt Clara and Becky sharing a cup of coffee at Becky's kitchen table.

Aunt Clara: Oh, Becky, I am so glad I met you at the Baptist Church. When I first came to Leavenworth, it was pretty scary. I had been a slave all of my life. My master had just died and my mistress had given me my freedom. I didn't know what I was going to do. My mistress gave me a letter that helped me get a job when I arrived here in Leavenworth.

Becky: I know what you mean, Clara. I was scared when I first got my freedom and opened my laundry business. It is doing well and things look good for me now. But, Clara, why did you want to come all the way from Kentucky to Kansas?

Clara: I guess I keep hoping I will find my daughter 'Liza Jane. I was separated from my family when my first master died and we were all sold. My new master tried to help me find out about my family. I know that my oldest daughter Margaret is dead and I think that both my husband and son are dead also. 'Liza Jane was just 11 years old when we were separated.

Becky: I know how hard it is to lose family like that. You sound like you are worried about 'Liza Jane. Is it because she was so young?

Clara: Well, partly. 'Liza Jane was a twin. Her sister drowned in the creek when the girls were only seven. 'Liza Jane blamed herself because she couldn't save Paulina Ann. She had nightmares all the time about it. I just pray that she is all right and that someday I can find her again. I save every penny I can in hopes that someday I can search for her.

Narrator: A year or so after Clara arrived in Kansas, she found out that the people she was working for were going to move. They asked Clara to go to California with them. She decided she would rather try to go to the Pikes Peak Territory. She hadn't been able to save enough money yet and she began wondering what she would do. Who else would she turn to but her good friend, Becky. Once again the two friends are having coffee at Becky's kitchen table.

Clara: What do you think I should do? I need to find work.

Becky: I have more customers than I can handle. I'll help you set up your own laundry if you want.

168

Clara: Becky, you always have the best ideas for me. Thank you.

Narrator: Becky did help Clara get set up in the laundry business. It was not long after this that Clara heard about a wagon train headed for the Pikes Peak Territory. She made arrangements to work her way there. She cooked and washed for 26 men. On June 8, 1859, Clara arrived in the Denver area. She got a job in a bakery and settled into life in Denver. Clara worked hard and invested some of her savings in houses and mining claims. By 1866, Clara had a good enough bank balance so she could plan a trip to Kentucky to look for 'Liza Jane. On her way back to Colorado, Clara stopped to see Becky. Let's listen as they talk.

Becky: Why don't you start at the beginning and tell me what has happened to you the past seven years.

Clara: I moved from Denver up to Central City. I began doing laundry for many of the miners. I've been told mine was the first laundry in the territory. When I got enough money I planned this trip to Kentucky. I hoped to find my 'Liza Jane. I couldn't find her, but I figured I had enough money to bring 16 freed slaves back to Colorado with me.

Narrator: Well, Clara took the 16 people, who were in need, home to Central City. She continued to help them until they had all found jobs and places to stay. This was not an unusual thing for Clara. She had always shared her food, her home and her clothing with anyone in need.

When she got back to Central City, Clara had a friend look into the cost of her trip. It seems that someone in Kansas had stolen more than $4,000 from her. Clara had very little money left. She continued to work as long as she could. She was almost eighty years old when she got so sick she could work no longer. Friends moved her to Denver. She needed to live at the lower altitude. One friend let her live in a house he owned, rent free, for the rest of her life. Other friends would bring food and money to help her. It was hard for Clara who had spent her whole life doing things for others to let others do things for her.

In 1881, Clara got a letter telling her that she was a certified member of the Society of Colorado Pioneers. This was not only because she was one of the first women to come to Colorado, but also because she was an outstanding citizen. This was a very special honor for her.

One day Clara got a letter from Becky. It told her that Becky

Clara Brown helped to start St. James Methodist Church in Central City. *(Credit: C.H.S.)*

thought she might have found 'Liza Jane. With the help of her friends, Clara was able to travel to Iowa where Becky was living. Clara went to see 'Liza Jane. Clara had a wonderful visit with her daughter and met her granddaughter for the first time. When Aunt Clara returned to Colorado, her granddaughter went with her and took care of her until Aunt Clara died in 1885.

Clara was active in starting **St. James Methodist Church** in Central City. It is one of the oldest churches in Colorado. It was organized in July of 1859. Services were held in the home of Aunt Clara Brown until the church building was completed in 1872. This church is still standing and has a plaque to honor Clara Brown.

The three girls turned toward the class and bowed. Everyone began to clap.

Emily Griffith

Maria, Zach, and Nicole came to the front of the room. Maria and Zach were carrying a large box. The words "TIME MACHINE" were written on the side of the box. Zach and Maria climbed into it. The time machine began to shake and roar. When it stopped, the two got out. Nicole was sitting at a desk working on some papers. She looked up as the two got out of the time machine.

"Where are we? What year is it?" Maria asked.

"Let's see," answered Zach looking at some dials on the side of his time machine. "It is 1928 and we are in Denver, Colorado." The two children walked over to the desk.

"Hello, my name is Maria and this is Zach. We are time travelers and we have come from the 21st century."

"I am **Emily Griffith** and I am very happy to meet you," said Nicole.

"Could we ask you some questions?" said Maria.

"I would be glad to answer as many of your questions as I can."

"Can you tell us something about your childhood?" asked Zach.

"Well, I was born in 1880. My family was very poor so I had to begin working at an early age. I started teaching school when I was just 14. I really had to read a lot to try to keep ahead of my students."

"When did you come to Colorado?" asked Maria.

"My family moved to Denver in 1904. I was 24 years old. My sister and I both got jobs as teachers. My sister always said that to be a good teacher you must learn as much about your students as you can. I always tried to do that."

"Can you tell us your favorite story about being a teacher?" asked Zach.

"I guess the story that comes to mind is the one that helped my dream come true. From the time I first began to teach, I had always dreamed of opening a school where anyone who wanted to learn could come. It would not matter how old someone was or what they wanted to learn. I hoped that this school would be for everyone.

Emily Griffith lived from 1880 until 1947.
(Credit: C.H.S.)

"Most of my students came from homes where there was not much money. I was worried that they would have very little for Christmas. The *Denver Post* ran an advertisement. They asked people to donate toys, clothes, books, and food to be given to poor children. The children had to go to the newspaper office to get their gifts. I knew that my students would not go unless someone took them. I went down there with all of my students. It took a full day to help all of them choose their gifts."

"How did that help your dream come true?" asked Zach.

"There was a newspaper reporter watching as I helped my children. She asked me for an interview. She found out how much I loved teaching and then I told her about my dream of a school where everyone, no matter how old, could come to learn. The reporter wrote a story about me and about my dream. In fact, she wrote several articles about it."

"What happened then?" asked Maria.

"The men who were in charge of the Denver Public Schools decided to let me have this building for my school. The building was not being used. It was old and dirty. Several of my teaching friends helped my sister and me scrub and paint.

We spent the whole summer getting the building ready. We put up signs all over Denver telling about our *Opportunity School*. The signs were in English and Spanish, as well as several other languages."

"When did you open your school?" asked Zach.

"The doors were first opened on September 9, 1916. There was only one small boy at our door, but by the end of the week more than 1,400 people had come to our new school. The Opportunity School is open from 8:30 in the morning till 9:30 at night."

"What kinds of things do you teach?" asked Maria.

"We teach reading, writing, and arithmetic. We also teach everything from auto mechanics and hair cutting to business and typing. At one time, we had 100 people who wanted to learn to type. We had only one typewriter. It took some real work to figure out a way so that everyone could learn to type."

"What is that wonderful smell?" asked Zach.

"That is my soup pot. I learned a long time ago that it is hard to learn if you are hungry. Many people come here right from work. They do not have time to stop for a meal. Others may not have enough money to buy food. That is why I try to keep a soup pot going all the time. It is there for anyone who is hungry."

"Why do you have your desk out here by the front door?" asked Maria.

"This makes it possible for me to keep track of everything that is happening in my school. I am very proud of my school. Thousands of people have come here to learn lots of different things."

People of all ages came to the Opportunity School to learn.
(Credit: C.H.S.)

"Thank you for the interview," said Zach. "We need to get back so we can share what we learned with our class."

Zach and Maria returned to the time capsule. Again it roared and shook. When they got out, they were back in their own classroom again. The three children sat down while the class clapped.

Helen Hunt Jackson

Kelsey came to the front of the class carrying a stack of books. She sat down at a table and began looking at one of the books. She started writing on a note pad. Then she put her head in her hands. She looked like she was going to cry. Just then Adam came to the front of the room. He walked over to Kelsey.

"Why do you look so sad?" he asked.

"Oh, hi, Adam," she answered. "I am trying to write a report about an author named *Helen Hunt Jackson*. She had so many unhappy things happen to her that it makes me sad to think about it."

"What kind of unhappy things happened to her?" asked Adam.

"She was an orphan by the age of 17. It would be really hard to lose your parents so young. She finished school and when she was 22, she married Edward Hunt. Their first child was a boy who died before his first birthday. A second child, Rennie, was born soon after that. Then her husband was killed in an accident. Rennie was all she had left. When Rennie was 9 both he and Helen got diphtheria. This is a really bad sickness. Rennie died and Helen was left alone."

Helen Hunt Jackson wrote several famous books.
(Credit: C.H.S.)

"Boy, she really did have a sad life," said Adam. "What happened next?"

"Helen began writing poetry. She felt that getting her thoughts and feelings down on paper helped her. Soon she began writing stories for newspapers and magazines. Then she began writing stories for children. Her stories were beginning to make her famous."

"It sounds like things were getting better for her. What brought her to Colorado?" asked Adam.

"Helen got sick and the doctor thought that the Colorado air would be good for her. Helen moved to *Colorado Springs*."

"Did she get better?" asked Adam.

"Yes, the air in Colorado did seem to help her feel better.

Colorado
Springs

173

Shortly after she moved to Colorado, she met a man named Mr. Jackson. He asked her to marry him. At first, she did not want to marry again because so many people she loved had died. Finally, she did marry him and became Helen Hunt Jackson."

"Did she still write?" asked Adam.

"Yes. She began learning about the Indians in Colorado. It really made her sad to learn how badly the Indians had been treated. She began telling people how the government had broken so many promises to them. She also began writing about it. At first, she wrote for newspapers, but finally she wrote a book called *A Century of Dishonor*. In this book, she told about some of the many promises to the Indians the government had broken."

"What else did she write?" asked Adam.

"She knew how much the book *Uncle Tom's Cabin* had helped black people," answered Kelsey. "She hoped to write a book that would help the Indians as much. She wrote about a beautiful Indian girl and her husband. The book told how they had lost their home, their land, and their way of life because the government kept breaking promises. The book was called *Ramona*. The story may have helped the Indians some, but not as much as she had hoped."

"It sounds like she was a great writer," said Adam. "I remember seeing a picture of her grave. It was up on **Cheyenne Mountain**. I heard that she asked her husband to bury her near **Seven Falls**. I guess lots of people thought she was a good writer. People kept coming to see her grave. Everyone who came would pile a big rock on top of it until there was a really large pile."

"You're right, Adam," said Kelsey. "I also read that the man who owned the land where she was buried began charging people 10 cents to go and see the grave. I guess this made Mr. Jackson mad. He had Helen's body moved to a quiet grave in Colorado Springs. She had lots of sad things happen to her, but she worked hard to try and help others."

"Good job," said Mr. Brown as Kelsey and Adam returned to their seats. "Who is next?"

Ben Nighthorse Campbell

Paul and Ed came to the front of the room. Paul was wearing slacks, a cowboy shirt, bolo tie, and cowboy boots. He was pretending to be **Ben Nighthorse Campbell**. Ed had a notepad and pencil in his hand.

"I know that you are pretty busy as a U.S. Senator, but I wondered if I could ask you a few questions?" asked Ed.

"Of course," he replied.

"Could you tell me about the early years of your life?" asked Ed.

"I was born in California on April 13, 1933. My mother had tuberculosis so she was sick much of the time. My father was sick also. He was an alcoholic. He wasn't home very much and my mother wasn't able to take care of my sister and me. By the time I was two years old, I was spending time in the St. Patrick's Children's Home."

"Do you have any other memories of your father?" asked Ed.

Ben Nighthorse Campbell is an Indian Chief and Colorado legislator.
(Credit: C.H.S.)

"Yes, I remember him showing me how to make Indian jewelry. My father was part Cheyenne. He had been treated badly by some people and he thought it was because he was Indian. He told me never to tell anyone that I was Indian because he didn't want me to be treated badly."

"I heard that you have held several jobs. Can you tell me what some of them were?" asked Ed.

"Actually, I started out as a street kid and delinquent. Then I became a soldier. I have also been a policeman, a teacher, a truck driver, a farmer, a judo instructor, and a jewelry maker. There are not too many people in public office who can say they have had that many different jobs."

"Tell me about your family," Ed said.

"My wife Linda and I were married in 1966. We have a daughter, Shanan, and a son, Colin."

"Where did you get the name Nighthorse?" asked Ed.

"I began learning as much as I could about the

Cheyenne. I wanted to know about my heritage. In 1976, I was invited to join the Northern Cheyenne. They gave me the name Nighthorse."

"What brought you to Colorado?" asked Ed.

"Both my son Colin and I have asthma. It was getting harder and harder to breathe where we lived. Linda was from Colorado and we had heard that Colorado air is good for people with asthma. In 1977, we bought a ranch in *Ignacio*. I continued to teach judo and make Indian jewelry. I started breeding quarter horses and kept up my hobby of riding motorcycles."

• Ignacio

"I heard that you went to the Olympics in 1964. Is that true?" asked Ed.

"Yes. I was captain of the 1964 Judo team in Japan. I was the U.S. Judo champion three times. I was a gold medal winner in the Pan-American games of 1963."

"When did you become active in politics?" asked Ed.

"In 1982, I went to a meeting to select candidates for the Democratic Party. No one wanted to run for the Colorado House of Representatives because the Republican candidate looked too strong. Someone asked me if I would run. No one thought I could win, but I did. After three years in the Colorado House of Representatives, I decided to run for the U.S. House of Representatives. Again, no one thought I would win, but I did. When I was sworn into office in January of 1987, I became the eighth Native American to serve in the U.S. House of Representatives."

"I understand you had a little problem with the dress code for the U.S. House of Representatives," said Ed.

"I asked them to let me dress more in line with my heritage. They voted to let me wear my boots and a bolo tie. I feel much more comfortable that way."

"When did you become an Indian chief?" asked Ed.

"In 1985, I was invited to sit on the council of chiefs. I was really honored."

"I understand you did not always vote the way other Democrats voted," said Ed.

"No, I have always voted the way I feel the people in my district and state would want me to vote."

"I heard you changed from being a Democrat to being a Republican. Why did you choose to do that?" asked Ed.

"For years I have voted as often with the Republicans as with the Democrats. Then I found that I was voting even more often with the Republicans. That is why in 1985, I decided to change parties."

"What made you decide to run for the Senate?" asked Ed.

"I had just been elected to my third term in the House of Representatives when I learned that **Tim Wirth** would not be running for the Senate in 1992. That is when I decided to run. It was a hard race, but I won. I was the first American Indian to serve in the Senate in more than 60 years. In 1998, I ran again for the Senate and won with 62% of the vote."

"Thank you, Mr. Campbell, for answering so many of my questions," concluded Ed. The boys returned to their seats, and Kate and Jessie went to the coatroom.

Many people called Margaret Brown "The Unsinkable Molly Brown."
(Credit: C.H.S.)

Margaret "Molly" Brown

The theme music from the film *The Titanic* floated into the classroom from the back of the room. Kate and Jessie looked like they were sitting in a cardboard rowboat. As they reached the front of the room they stopped rowing.

"We're safe! We're safe!" exclaimed Kate. "The way you took over and helped us get organized made all the difference. I think we might have frozen to death if you had not made us take turns rowing. You kept our spirits up too by getting us to sing. Thank you, Mrs. Brown."

"Please call me Margaret. I really didn't do anything." Kate held up a sign that said, "THREE WEEKS LATER."

"I am so glad to see you again, Margaret," said Kate. "I can't believe all the things that have happened to us the past few weeks."

"Yes, it has been quite an experience finding out the unsinkable *Titanic* really was sinkable. The time we spent in that lifeboat and then aboard the rescue ship, *Carpathia*, was an experience I don't want to repeat."

"Margaret, it was wonderful the way you helped nurse the people on the rescue ship," said Kate. "I also heard that since we got back, you have been helping a lot of the people who lost everything on the *Titanic*."

"Well, I feel lucky that I was able to help some people."

"I would really like to get to know you better. Would you please tell me a little bit about yourself?" said Kate. "Where were you born?"

"I was born in Hannibal, Missouri, in 1867. I now live in Colorado."

"What was it like when you first got to Colorado?" asked Kate.

"I was just 19 years old when my brother and I came to Colorado on the train. We were hoping to make our fortune in the gold mines. When we came to **Leadville,** it was a rough mining town. There were thousands of men, but not very many women. I got a job sewing and putting carpets together for a store."

"Tell me about your husband," said Kate.

"I fell in love with J.J. shortly after I came to Leadville. He was a manager of a mine. We went through some really hard times for a while, but J.J. found a way to dig mines deeper and safer. When he hit gold, we became millionaires."

"What kinds of things do you like to do?" asked Kate.

"I love to read. There are so many things I want to learn. I love to travel to see some of the places I had read about. I have learned to speak five languages."

"I understand you have worked for women's rights," said Kate.

"Yes, I have always thought that women should have as much right to vote as men. I also think that women should be allowed to fight alongside men if they want to. Not many people agree with me, but I feel women should have the same rights as men."

"The newspapers are calling you the '**Unsinkable Molly Brown**'. Were you called Molly when you were little?" asked Kate.

"No, I was called Maggie until I was about 12. After that I was always called Margaret."

"Why don't you let them know your name is not Molly?" asked Kate.

"I really don't mind what they call me. They have written a lot of really funny stories about me. Someone wrote that once when J.J. brought home the payroll for the mine that I hid the money in the wood stove. Then when J.J. came home he lit a fire and burned up over $300,000.

"Most of the stories they tell are not true. I don't say anything because it makes a good story. The tales about me keep getting bigger and bigger. Its pretty funny. I just have a good laugh."

Kate and Jessie returned to their seats.

"That was our last group. I think every group did an excellent job!" exclaimed Mr. Brown. "I hope you have learned as much as I have about some of the people who have been important to Colorado. There are a lot more interesting people. You may want to learn about some of them on your own."

What Did You Learn?

1. What was the other professional sport that John Elway thought about playing?

2. Who was the only astronaut to also be an aquanaut?

3. Who was Denver's first Hispanic mayor?

4. How did Horace Tabor first make his fortune?

5. Who was the world heavyweight boxing champion from 1919-1926?

6. Who was nicknamed the "Man of a Thousand Faces?"

7. Name two tragedies in Helen Hunt Jackson's life.

8. Who started the first laundry in Colorado?

9. Which famous person in this chapter could speak five languages?

10. Which famous person from this chapter has a statue in the United States Statuary Hall?

11. Which U.S. Representative from Colorado got Congress to change their dress code?

12. What did Emily Griffith do to help people in Colorado?

What Do You Think?

1. If you could have something named after you, what would you choose?   Why?

2. If you could become any one of the famous people talked about in this chapter, who would you choose? Why?

3. Who are some famous people from your area?

Use Your Imagination

1. You have just become very famous. Tell your life story. How did you become famous? What special thing did you do?

2. Your teacher has just told you that you are going to interview the governor of Colorado. What questions would you ask?

Conclusion
Rendezvous

It was a bright sunny Thursday. All of the students in Mr. Brown's class were counting the number of days until summer. They were all talking about special plans for their vacations.

"I hate to interrupt you," said Mr. Brown, "but before you go home, I just want to remind you about our Rendezvous tomorrow." The students all stopped talking.

"Will it be like one the mountain men went to?" asked Kelsey.

"Well, something like that," answered Mr. Brown. "I want all of you to dress up like you were on your way to a rendezvous in the 1800s. There will be many things for you to see, hear, and do. All of the activities will have to do with Colorado's history. It will be a really fun day. I hope you will all enjoy the things that we have planned. It is time to go home now. I will see you tomorrow."

Mountain men showed the students long rifles at the Rendezvous.

The next day the students all arrived dressed in costumes. They were looking forward to their Rendezvous. Mr. Brown took them out to a large field behind the school. First, they heard all about the life of a mountain man. The men showed the students some real beaver traps and tools used by mountain men. Next they watched some Indian dancers perform. Everyone was really impressed. Two

Pike and Long talked about their expeditions.

Gold panning was a favorite activity for many of the fourth graders.

men dressed like Pike and Long were there. They shared some of the things that happened on their expeditions.

After lunch, the students broke up into smaller groups and rotated through several centers. They learned how to pan for gold, square dance, and saw wood. They played some old fashioned games and ate jerky at the Country Store. The stagecoach and covered wagon rides were the favorite activities. When the students returned to the classroom, they were still bubbling with excitement.

"That was the best day I have ever had!" exclaimed Jessie.

"Me, too," agreed Gania.

"Can we do it again next week?" asked Kelsey.

"I wish we could, but it is the last week of school. We have a lot of things to do," said Mr. Brown. "Right now, it is almost time to go home. I am glad you had a good time at the Rendezvous. It is a great way to end a wonderful year."

"But I don't want it to end, Mr. Brown," said Maria.

"It has been fun," agreed Mr. Brown. "We have learned many things about our great state. Let's take a minute to talk about some of the things we have learned.

"We learned that Colorado has many special symbols. These symbols are all things that are important to our state," said Mr. Brown.

"My favorite symbol is the lark bunting," said Nicole.

"That is a wonderful symbol," agreed Mr. Brown. "We also learned about landforms. Can anyone name one of the landforms found in Colorado?"

"Mountains," said Keith. "I'll always remember that **Mt. Elbert** is the tallest mountain in Colorado."

"Great memory," praised Mr. Brown. "As you remember, the American Indians were the first people to live in Colorado. Who were some of the first American explorers?"

asked Mr. Brown.

"*Zebulon Pike* and *Stephen Long*," remembered Brink.

"You're right. Who came here after them?" asked Mr. Brown.

"The mountain men," answered Yeong Se.

"Why did the mountain men come to Colorado?" asked Mr. Brown.

"They wanted to trap beaver," said Abigail.

"Super! Who remembers what happened in 1858 that brought a lot of people to Colorado in 1859?" asked Mr. Brown.

Mr. Brown and his students had fun square dancing at the Rendezvous.

"Gold was discovered!" exclaimed Zach.

"That's right," said Mr. Brown. "That helped Colorado to become a territory and eventually a state. Unfortunately, all of these people coming to Colorado also caused many problems between the settlers and the American Indians."

"I wish the settlers and the Indians could have gotten along better," said Abigail. "Then there might not have been any wars in Colorado."

"That would have been nice," agreed Mr. Brown. "Eventually things did settle down. Colorado's industries started to grow. Many people came to Colorado and helped it become the great state it is today."

"We are lucky to live in Colorado," said Chelsea.

"I agree," said Mr. Brown. "Colorado is a great state with many things to offer. There is so much to learn about Colorado."

"I wish we didn't have to stop learning about Colorado history," said Lindsay.

"You never have to stop," stated Mr. Brown. "I have been teaching about Colorado for over ten years now. Every year I learn something new. Each night on the news, things are happening that will become a part of our history. I hope you will keep reading and learning about Colorado. It is a wonderful state. And you have been a super class. I am going to miss all of you this summer. I hope you will come to see me next year."

183

"We will," said the class together. "You are a great teacher!"

The following week went very quickly. On the last day of school, everyone was excited about summer. They were also sad to leave all of their friends. They decided it was kind of like saying goodbye at a rendezvous. It was hard to say goodbye, but they knew they would see their friends at the next rendezvous.

"Have a great summer!"

"See you next year!"

Happy Trails! See you at the next rendezvous!

Glossary

Adobe: A building material made by mixing clay, sand, water, and straw. This mixture can then be formed into bricks and dried.

Agriculture: Another word for farming or raising crops or animals.

Alpine tundra: The area at the top of a mountain where the growing period is only about five or six weeks. Trees cannot grow in this area.

Amphitheater: A rising row of seats around an open space.

Arastra: (uh-RAS-truh) Used by miners to crush ore. It is a round hole lined with rocks. A drag stone was pulled around inside the hole to crush the ore against the stones.

Archaeologists: Scientists who study about people who lived a long time ago.

Arroyo: A dry gully.

Atlatl: (AT-a-lat-ul) A stick-like tool that was used to help hunters throw their spears with greater force.

Ball mills: Hollow iron balls used to break up ore. Ore and small metal balls were placed inside the large hollow balls. As they turned on a shaft, the pellets hit the ore and broke it up into smaller pieces.

Bear Dance: A traditional Ute Indian dance that symbolizes the beginning of new life in the spring.

Brands: A shape or design that is burned into the hair of an animal with a hot iron. Each ranch has a special design to show which animals belong to that ranch.

Bullwhacker: Name of the driver of a wagon pulled by oxen.

Cache: (KASH) A hiding place where fur trappers stored their furs.

Canyon: A long narrow valley with steep sides.

Castor or castoreum: (kas-TOR-ee-uhm) A liquid that comes from a beaver. The mountain men used it as bait on their beaver traps.

Centennial: The celebration of a 100 year anniversary.

Cholera: (KOL-er-ah) A bad disease or sickness that spreads from one person to another. It often comes from drinking bad water.

Claim clubs: The farmers in an area wrote the laws or rules the people in the area agreed to live by. They also chose a group of people who would help to settle arguments.

Climate: The type of weather usually found in an area.

Colony settlement: A group of people worked together to build their town and farm their land.

Company town: A town where the houses and stores were all owned by the mining company.

Constitution: A paper that lists the laws or rules everyone will live by.

Constitutional convention: A meeting where a constitution is written.

Continental Divide: An imaginary line that runs along the highest point of the Rocky Mountains. All the water on the west side runs toward the Pacific Ocean and water on the east side runs toward the Atlantic.

Cradleboard: Used by the Indian women to carry babies on their backs. The baby is laid on a hard board and then held in place with material.

Cradle rocker: A box placed on rockers. It was used to help separate gold from sand and gravel.

Culture: The way in which a group of people lived at any one time.

Customs: The things people do, that people before them also did a long time ago.

Drafts: Pieces of paper that were used like a check or an I.O.U. It was a promise that the government would pay that amount of money.

Drought: A time when there is very little rainfall and water is scarce.

Dry farming: Farming that does not use irrigation but depends on the natural rainfall to water the crops.

Elevation: (el-uh-VAY-shun) The number of feet above sea level, or the height of the land above sea level.

Erode: (ee-RODE) The process of wind or rain wearing away the rocks or land.

Extinct: A living thing that no longer exists. Something which would no longer be living on this earth.

Feeder tracks: Railroad tracks that helped to connect towns with the transcontinental railroad.

Fissure: A deep crack or cut in the surface of the ground.

Flume: A long box that is used like a ditch to carry water from a river or stream to where it is needed. The miners used flumes to bring water to their mining sites.

Foothills: Hills near the bottom or foot of a mountain.

Freight wagons: Large wagons used to carry heavy loads. Often two or three wagons would be fastened together and pulled by one large team.

Gold dust: Tiny flecks of gold.

Gorge: (Gorje) A deep narrow opening between steep cliffs.

Grubstake: Food, money, and supplies were given to a miner to use while he searched for gold. If the miner found gold, he had to share it with the person who gave him the grubstake.

Hard rock mining: Drilling holes or tunnels into the side of a cliff or mountain to find ore or minerals.

Headwaters: The headwaters of a river is the source or beginning point of a river.

Hill: An area of high land which is lower than a mountain.

Hopper: A box with holes in the bottom of it that was placed on top of a cradle rocker. This box held the sand and gravel.

Hydraulic mining: (Hi-DRAH-lick) A stream of water was shot through a pipe or hose. This was used to break up the soil so it was easier to find gold or silver.

Ice Age: A time when it was so cold that even the rivers froze. Ice and snow covered large areas of land.

Industries: Businesses like farming, manufacturing and mining are all industries.

Irrigation: (ir-uh-GAY-shuhn) Supplying farm land with water from another place. The water usually flows through ditches or pipes.

Jerky: (JER-kee) Meat that has been sliced into thin strips and dried.

Kiva: A round room that was partially sunk into the ground. The kiva was usually used only by the men and boys for religious ceremonies.

Lake: Large body of water surrounded by land.

Landforms: Things like mountains, valleys, and rivers that give the earth its shape.

Latitude: (LAT-i-tood) Imaginary lines that run east and west around the earth. These lines are parallel to the equator. They are used to help find a special place on a map.

Legend: (LEJ-uhnd) A story or group of stories that have been handed down from one generation to the next. They are often based on history.

Legislature: (LEJ-is-lay-chur) Men and women elected by the people of the state to make laws and decisions about how the state should be run.

Lode mining: Digging underground or into a cliff or mountainside to find metals such as gold or silver. It is sometimes called hard rock mining or underground mining.

Longitude: (LONJ-i-tood) Imaginary lines that run north and south on the earth. They divide the earth into sections. This makes it easier to find a special place on a map.

Mammoth: A very large hairy elephant like animal that lived millions of years ago.

Mano and metate: (MAH-no and muh-TAH-tay) The mano is a round rock that was rubbed over a metate or flat rock to grind food.

Mercury: A heavy liquid metal that attracts gold.

Mining districts: The miners in an area chose someone to keep a record of all the mining claims. They also made a list of rules that everyone agreed to live by.

Mining town: A town where miners lived.

Molybdenum: An element mined in Colorado that is used to harden steel.

Morache: (MORE-awch) A musical instrument used by the Ute in their bear dance. It is sometimes called a growler because it makes a sound like a bear growling.

Mountain: A natural raised part of the earth larger than a hill.

Mountain Range: A row or group of mountains.

Mucker: A person who shoveled dirt from the mines.

Muleskinner: A person who drove a wagon pulled by mules.

Nomadic: People who do not live in one place, but travel around in search of food.

Nuggets: Pieces of gold the size of a piece of rice or corn or sometimes even larger.

Open range: An area where animals graze together. There are no fences to keep each person's animals separate.

Ore: Rock that has a valuable metal, like gold or silver, in it.

Pack Train: A group of horses or mules carrying heavy packs. They were often fastened together in long lines. Each horse or mule could carry up to two hundred and fifty pounds of freight.

Park: High, level land surrounded by mountain ranges.

Pemmican: (PEM-i-kuhn) Dried meat that has been ground into a fine powder, mixed with melted fat, and formed into little cakes. Sometimes berries are added to the cakes.

Petroglyph: (PET-roh-glif) Symbols or pictures scratched or carved into rock.

Pictograph: (PIK-toh-graf) A symbol or picture painted on the rocks.

Pit house: A house built in a pit about 4 feet deep. The sides were made of poles and covered with mud. The door was a hole in the flat roof. A ladder was used to get in and out of the pit house.

Placer mining: (PLAS-er) Mining for gold that is in the sand or gravel on or near the surface of the earth.

Plains: A large area of flat land. This is often excellent farm land.

Plateau: An area of high flat land often with one or more very steep sides or cliffs.

Plew: (PLOO) The name the mountain men called a beaver skin or fur. It is the American spelling of the French word "plus" which means pelt.

Precipitation: (pre-sip-i-TAY-shuhn) Rain, snow, or other types of moisture that fall from the sky.

Prospectors: People who are looking or searching for something like gold or silver.

Providence: Divine guidance or care.

Pueblo: Houses grouped together like a town. They were often stacked several stories high.

Quarantine: A time when people or animals are kept separate from others to help prevent the spread of disease.

Rendezvous: (RON-day-voo) A French word for "place of meeting." A meeting of the fur trappers and traders in order to trade furs for supplies.

Reservation: Area set aside as a place for the Indians to live.

Reservoir: A place where water is collected and stored for use.

Riffles: Bars of wood fastened to the bottom of a box to help trap the heavy gold as the sand and gravel are washed away.

River: A natural stream of water flowing into a lake or ocean.

Roundup: When cattle on the open range are gathered together.

Scrip: A piece of paper that could be used to purchase supplies at the company store. Miners were often paid in scrip rather than money.

Shinny: A game played by teams of 10-25 women. The object of the game was to move the ball by kicking or hitting it with a stick to the opponent's goal.

Sign language: The hands and arms are placed in different ways to form signs for words or phrases.

Sinew: (SIN-noo) A tendon that fastens the muscle to the bone. The sinew of an animal was used for many things.

Sipapu: (SEE-pah-pu) A hole in the bottom of a kiva that represents an entrance from the lower spiritual world.

Sluice box: (SLOOS) A long box with bars or riffles spaced along the bottom. The box is placed at a slant. Sand and gravel are shoveled in at the high end. Water washes the sand and gravel out leaving gold trapped behind the riffles.

Stagecoach: An early form of travel. These wagons or coaches carried passengers and mail. They also often carried gold and silver.

Stamp mill: A machine that crushes ore to get out the valuable metals.

Strike: When union workers refuse to work until they get the salary or working conditions they demand.

Supply towns: These were larger towns that provided supplies to many of the mining towns or camps.

Swing station: A place where the stagecoach could stop to get fresh horses and drivers.

Symbol: A picture, object or action that stands for something else.

Telegraph: A system for sending messages by code over wires.

Territory: Part of the United States that has not yet become a state. It has a governor and a legislature.

Tipi: Sometimes spelled tepee. An Indian tent made from poles and covered with animal skins or woven mats. Tipis were shaped like an upside down ice cream cone.

Toll: Fee charged for permission to travel over a bridge or on a road.

Transcontinental railroad: A railroad that would go from coast to coast across the country.

Travois: (trav-OY) The ends of two long poles were fastened on either side of a horse or dog. The other ends of the pole dragged on the ground. A skin was stretched and fastened between the poles. The travois was used to help carry heavy things.

Treeline: Trees do not grow above this elevation on a mountain.

Tributary: Small river that flows into a larger river.

Tuberculosis: A disease of the lungs which makes breathing very hard.

Underground Mining: Drilling holes or tunnels into the side of a cliff or mountain to find ore or minerals.

Union: A group formed to help protect the rights of workers.

Uranium: An element mined in Colorado that is used for nuclear energy.

Valley: The low land that lies between hills or mountains.

Vein: A strip or section in a mountain that is almost pure gold.

Wickiup: A shelter made with branches, brush or hides. Sometimes it was built like a lean-to against a tree and at other times it was a tipi shaped shelter made with poles.

Index

Abbott, Carl, <u>A History of the Centennial State</u>. Boulder CO: Colorado Associated University Press, 1976.

Andersen, T.J., <u>John Elway</u>. Mankato, Minnesota: Crestwood House, 1988.

Arnold, Caroline, <u>The Ancient Cliff Dwellers of Mesa Verde</u>. New York: Clarion Books, 1992.

Ayer, Eleanor H., <u>The Anasazi</u>. New York: Walker and Company, 1993.

Ayer, Eleanor H., <u>Celebrate the States-Colorado</u>. New York: Benchmark Books Marshall Cavendish, 1997.

Basque, Garnet, <u>Methods of Placer Mining</u>. Langley, B.C.: Mr. Paperback, 1983.

Blair, Edward and E. Richard Churchill, <u>Everybody Came to Leadville</u>. Leadville, CO: Timberline Books, 1971.

Bledsoe, Sara, <u>Colorado</u>. Lerner Publications Company, 1993.

Bollinger, Edward T. and Frederick Bauer, <u>The Moffat Road</u>. Chicago: Sage Books, The Swallow Press, Inc., 1962.

Bonvillian, Nancy, <u>The Cheyennes</u>. Brookfield CT: The Millbrook Press, 1996.

Bowles, Samuel, <u>The Parks and Mountains of Colorado</u>. Norman, Oklahoma: University of Oklahoma Press, 1991.

Brown, Mary L.T. <u>Gems for the Taking</u>. New York, New York: Macmillan Company, 1971.

Brown, Robert L., <u>An Empire of Silver</u>. Caldwell, Idaho: Caxton Printers, Ltd.,1965.

Bruyn, Kathleen, <u>Aunt Clara Brown</u>. Boulder, CO: Pruett Publishing Company, 1970.

Bueler, Gladys R., <u>Colorado's Colorful Characters</u>. Boulder, CO: Pruett Publishing Company, 1981.

Burby, Liza N., <u>The Pueblo Indians</u>. New York: Chelsea Juniors, 1994.

Burk, John, <u>The Legend of Baby Doe</u>. New York: G.P. Putnam's Sons, 1974.

Carpenter, Allan, <u>The New Enchantment of America, Colorado</u>. Chicago: Childrens Press, 1978.

Catalano, Julie and Sandra Stotsky, <u>The Mexican Americans</u>. New York/

Philadelphia, 1996.

Catchpole, Dr. Clive, <u>Mountains</u>. New York: Dial Books for Young Readers E.P. Dutton, Inc., 1984.

Chamblin, Thomas S., Editor, <u>The Historical Encyclopedia of Colorado</u>. Colorado Historical Association.

Collinson, Alan,. <u>Ecology Watch Grasslands</u>. New York: Dillon Press, 1992.

Cory, Steven, <u>Pueblo Indian</u>. Minneapolis, Minnesota: Lerner Publications, Company, 1996.

Crum, Josie Moore, <u>Three Little Lines</u>. Durango, Colorado: Durango Herald-News, 1960.

Crutchfield, James A., <u>It Happened in Colorado</u>. Helena Montana: Falcon Press Publishing Co., Inc., 1993.

Dempsey, Jack and Barbara Piattelli Dempsey, <u>Jack Dempsey</u>. New York: Harper & Row, 1977.

Downey, Matthew T. and Fay D. Metcalf,. <u>Colorado: Crossroads of the West</u>. Boulder, CO: Pruett Publishing Company, 1986.

Doherty, Craig A. and Katherine M. Doherty, <u>The Ute</u>. Vero Beach, FL: Rourke Publications, Inc. 1994.

Drago, Harry Sinclair, <u>The Great Range Wars Violence on the Grasslands</u>. New York: Dodd, Mead & Company, 1970.

Fernandez-Shaw, Carlos, <u>The Hispanic Presence in North America</u>. New York: Facts on File, 1987.

Ferril, Thomas Hornsby, <u>Nothing is Long Ago A Documentary History of Colorado 1776-1976</u>. Denver Public Library, 1975.

Fox, Larry, <u>Sports Great John Elway</u>. Enslow Publishers, Inc. 1990.

Fradin, Dennis Brindell, <u>From Sea to Shining Sea</u>. Colorado/ Chicago: Childrens Press, 1994.

Freeman, Dona, Editor, <u>100 Years Montrose, CO.</u> 1982.

Fradin, Dennis B., <u>The Cheyenne</u>. Chicago: Children's Press, 1988.

Gregory, Marvin and P. David Smith,. <u>The Million Dollar Highway.</u> Wayfinder Press, 1986.

Hafen, LeRoy R. Editor, <u>Mountain Men & Fur Traders of the Far West</u>. Lincoln/London: University of Nebraska Press, 1972.

Hart, Janice, Editor, "Spanish & Mexican Land Grants in Colorado". <u>Colorado Fever.</u> Volume 1 #6.

Henry, Christopher, <u>Ben Nighthorse Campbell Cheyenne Chief & U.S. Senator</u>. Philadelphia -New York: Chelsea House Publishers, 1994.

Hill, William E., <u>The Santa Fe Trail Yesterday & Today</u>. Caldwell, ID: Caxton Printers, Ltd., 1992.

Hofsinde, Robert, <u>Indian Games and Crafts</u>. New York: William Morrow and Company, 1957.

Hofsinde, Robert, <u>The Indian and the Buffalo</u>. New York: William Morrow and Company, 1961.

Hoig, Stan, <u>The Cheyenne</u>. Philadelphia: Chelsea House Publishers, 1989.

Hoyt-Goldsmith, Diane, <u>Pueblo Storyteller</u>. New York: Holiday House, 1991.

Kaye, Judith, <u>The Life of Florence Sabin</u>. New York: Twenty-First Century Books Holt & Company, 1993.

Keen, Jerry, <u>Gold Prospectors Digest</u>. Northridge, CA: Keen Engineering Inc. 1996.

Kent, Deborah, <u>America the Beautiful</u>. Chicago: Childrens Press, 1989.

Kronstadt, Janet, <u>Florence Sabin, Medical Researcher</u>. New York: Chelsea House Publishers, 1990.

Lavender, David, <u>Bent's Fort</u>. New York: Doubleday & Company, Inc., 1957.

Linn, William Alexander, <u>Horace Greeley</u>: D. Appleton & Company, 1903.

Marcus, Rebecca B. <u>The First Book of Cliff Dwellers</u>. New York, New York: Franklin Watts, Inc., 1968.

Martell, Hazel Mary, <u>Native Americans and Mesa Verde</u>. New York: Dillon Press, 1993.

McMarrow, Catherine, <u>Gold Fever</u>. New York: Random House, 1996.

Metcalf, Fay D, Noel, Thomas J., Smith, Duane A., <u>Colorado, Heritage of the Highest State</u>. Boulder, CO: Pruett Publishing Company, 1984.

Monnett, John H. and Michael McCarthy, <u>Colorado Profiles</u>. Cordillera Press, Inc., 1987.

Mutel, Cornelia Fleischer and John C. Emerick, <u>Grassland to Glacier</u>. Boulder, CO: Johnson Books, 1992.

Myers, Arthur, <u>The Cheyenne</u>. New York: Franklin Watts, 1982.

Petersen, David, <u>Dinosaur National Monument</u>. Chicago: Childrens Press, 1995.

Petersen, David, <u>Rocky Mountain National Park</u>. Chicago: Childrens Press, 1993.

Petit, Jan, <u>Utes, The Mountain People</u>. Boulder: Johnson Books, 1990.

Petralia, J.F. <u>Gold Gold! Beginners Handbook. How to Prospect for Gold.</u> 1980.

Rachlis, Eugene, <u>Indians of the Plains</u>. American Heritage Publishing Co, Inc., 1960.

Radlauer, Ruth, <u>Mesa Verde National Park</u>. Chicago: Childrens Press, 1977.

Salomon, Julian Harris, <u>The Book of Indian Crafts and Indian Lore</u>. New York: Harper & Brothers Publishers. 1928.

Sattler, Helen Roney <u>The Earliest Americans</u>. New York: Clarion Books, 1993.

Savage, Jeff, <u>Gold Miners of the Wild West</u>. Enslow Publishers, Inc., 1995.

Shemie, Bonnie, <u>Houses of Adobe</u>. Tundra Books, 1995.

Shirley, Gayle C. <u>Four-Legged Legends of Colorado</u>. Helena Montana: Falcon Press Publishing Co., Inc., 1994.

Smith-Baranzini, Marlene and Howard Egger-Bouer, <u>American Indians</u>. Boston/New York: Little, Brown and Company, 1994.

Sneve, Virginia Driving Hawk, <u>The Apaches</u>. New York: Holiday House, 1997.

Spies, Karen, <u>Denver</u>. Minneapolis, MN: Dillon Press, Inc., 1988.

Sprague, Marshall, <u>Colorado</u>. New York: W.W. Norton & Company, Inc., 1976.

Stewart, Ron, <u>Dinosaurs of the West</u>. Missoula, MT: Mountain Press Publishing Co., 1998.

Stone, Lynn M., <u>Mountains</u>. Chicago: Childrens Press, 1983.

Teeuwen, Randall, Editor, <u>La Cultura Constante de San Luis</u>. Copyright by the San Luis Museum Cultural and Commercial Center, 1985.

Viola, Herman J., <u>Ben Nighthorse Campbell</u>. Orion Books, 1993.

Webb, Michele, Editor, <u>The Colorado Quick-Fact Book</u>. (Compiled by the Midwest Research Institute) Topeka, Kansas: Capper Press, 1992.

Weiss, Harvey, <u>Shelters From Tepee to Igloo</u>. New York: Thomas Y. Crowell, 1994.

Wenger, Gilbert R., <u>The Story of Mesa Verde National Park</u>. Mesa Verde Museum Association, Inc., 1993.

Wetridge Young Writer's Workshop, <u>Kids Explore America's Hispanic Heritage</u>. Santa Fe, NM: John Muir Publications, 1992.

Whitaker, Rosemary, <u>Helen Hunt Jackson</u>. Boise, ID: Boise State University, 1987.

Wilkes, Angela, <u>Mountains</u>. Usborne Publishing, Ltd., 1980.

Wills, Charles A., <u>A Historical Album of Colorado</u>. Brookfield, C T. Millbrook Press, 1996.

Zugelder, Ann, <u>LaVeta Hotel.</u> Gunnison, CO: B & B Printers, 1990.